First World War
and Army of Occupation
War Diary
France, Belgium and Germany

18 DIVISION
Divisional Troops
84 Brigade Royal Field Artillery
20 February 1915 - 28 December 1916

WO95/2025/2

The Naval & Military Press Ltd
www.nmarchive.com
Published in association with The National Archives

Published by

The Naval & Military Press Ltd

Unit 10 Ridgewood Industrial Park,

Uckfield, East Sussex,

TN22 5QE England

Tel: +44 (0) 1825 749494

www.naval-military-press.com

www.nmarchive.com

This diary has been reprinted in facsimile from the original. Any imperfections are inevitably reproduced and the quality may fall short of modern type and cartographic standards.

© **Crown Copyright**
Images reproduced by permission of The National Archives, London, England, 2015.

Contents

Document type	Place/Title	Date From	Date To
Heading	WO95/2025 18 Division Divisional Troops 84 Brigade Royal Field Artillery Jul 1915-Dec 1916		
Heading	18th Division 84th Bde R.F.A. Jly 1915-Dec 1916 To 4 Army		
Heading	War Diary 84th Brigade R.F.A. 18 Div Arty		
Heading	18th Division 84th Brigade R.F.A. Vol. I. 1-31-7-15 Dec 16		
War Diary	Oosthove Farm	01/07/1916	07/07/1916
War Diary	Oosthove Farm B 11d 36 Sheet 36 (3 Series) 1/20000	07/07/1916	08/07/1916
War Diary	Oosthove Farm	08/07/1916	23/07/1916
War Diary	Oosthove Farm B.11d.4.7	23/07/1916	24/07/1916
War Diary	Oosthove Farm	25/07/1916	31/07/1916
Diagram etc	Identification Trace for use with Artillery Maps.		
War Diary	Oosthove Farm		
Diagram etc	Identification Trace for use with Artillery Maps. Appendix 5		
Heading	18th Division 84th Brigade R.F.A. Vol II From 31 July to 31 aug 15		
War Diary	Coisy	31/07/1915	01/08/1915
War Diary	Heilly	02/08/1915	03/08/1915
War Diary	Bray	04/08/1915	06/08/1915
War Diary	Bronfay	08/08/1915	14/08/1915
War Diary	Bronfay Farm (Near Bray)	15/08/1915	21/08/1915
War Diary	Bronfay Farm	22/08/1915	25/08/1915
War Diary	Meaulte	26/08/1915	31/08/1915
Heading	18th Division 84th Bde. R.F.A. Amm Col Vol I August 15		
War Diary	Coisy	01/08/1915	01/08/1915
War Diary	Heilly	02/08/1915	04/08/1915
War Diary	Etinehem	05/08/1915	25/08/1915
War Diary	Treux	26/08/1915	31/08/1915
War Diary	Southampton.	26/08/1915	26/08/1915
War Diary	Harve	27/08/1915	27/08/1915
War Diary	Longueau	28/08/1915	28/08/1915
War Diary	Coisy	29/08/1915	31/08/1915
Heading	18th Division "A"/84 Battery R.F.A. Vol. I From 20 Jly to 5 aug 15		
War Diary	Heytesbury	20/07/1915	20/07/1915
War Diary	Warminster	26/07/1915	26/07/1915
War Diary	Harve	27/07/1915	28/07/1915
War Diary	Amiens	28/07/1915	29/07/1915
War Diary	Coisy	30/07/1915	01/08/1915
War Diary	Heilly	02/08/1915	03/08/1915
War Diary	Meaulte	04/08/1915	31/08/1915
War Diary	Coisy	30/07/1915	02/08/1915
War Diary	Heilly	03/08/1915	03/08/1915
War Diary	Meaulte	04/08/1915	05/08/1915
Heading	18th Division "B"/84 Battery R.F.A. Vol. I from 20 jly to 31 aug 15		
War Diary	Heytesbury	20/07/1915	26/07/1915

War Diary	Havre	27/07/1915	27/07/1915
War Diary	Longeau Coisy	28/07/1915	28/07/1915
War Diary	Coisy	02/08/1915	02/08/1915
War Diary	Heilly	02/08/1915	04/08/1915
War Diary	Bray	05/08/1915	07/08/1915
War Diary	Bronfay Farm Nr Bray	08/08/1915	14/08/1915
War Diary	Bray	14/08/1915	21/08/1915
War Diary	Bronfay Farm	20/08/1915	25/08/1915
War Diary	Meaulte	26/08/1915	27/08/1915
War Diary	2300 Yds E SE of Meaulte	28/08/1915	31/08/1915
Heading	18th Division "C"/84 Battery R.F.A. Vol. I. From 26 Jly To 31 Aug 15		
War Diary	Heytesbury	26/07/1915	26/07/1915
War Diary	Southampton	26/07/1915	26/07/1915
War Diary	Havre	27/07/1915	28/07/1915
War Diary	Longpre	29/07/1915	29/07/1915
War Diary	Coisy	29/07/1915	02/08/1915
War Diary	Heilly	03/08/1915	03/08/1915
War Diary	Bray	04/08/1915	05/08/1915
War Diary	E.N.E. Bray	06/08/1915	24/08/1915
War Diary	Meulte	25/08/1915	25/08/1915
War Diary	Meulte	26/08/1915	31/08/1915
Heading	18th Division "D"/84 Battery R.F.A. Vol. I from 20 Feb 31 aug 15		
War Diary	Heytesbury	20/02/1915	26/02/1915
War Diary	Harve	27/07/1915	29/07/1915
War Diary	Coisy	30/07/1915	02/08/1915
War Diary	Heilly	05/08/1915	05/08/1915
War Diary	Buire	06/08/1915	06/08/1915
War Diary	Suzanne	07/08/1915	25/08/1915
War Diary	Meaulte	25/08/1915	25/08/1915
War Diary	Suzanne	25/08/1915	25/08/1915
War Diary	Meaulte	26/08/1915	31/08/1915
Heading	18th Division 84th Brigade R.F.A. Vol. 3 Sept 15		
War Diary	Meaulte	01/09/1915	17/09/1915
War Diary	Meaulte and Albert	23/09/1915	30/09/1915
War Diary	Treux	30/09/1915	30/09/1915
Miscellaneous	G.S. XVIII Division. Mining Report, Tambour Du Clos.	17/09/1915	17/09/1915
Heading	18th Division 84th Bde. R.F.A. Vol 4 Oct 15		
War Diary	Meault	19/10/1915	22/10/1915
War Diary	Meault	21/10/1915	21/10/1915
Heading	18th Division 84th Bde. R.F.A. Vol 5 Nov 15		
War Diary	Meaulte	01/12/1915	01/12/1915
Heading	18th Division 84th Bde. R.F.A. Vol 6 Dec 15		
War Diary	Meaulte	17/12/1915	30/12/1915
Heading	18th Div 84th Bde R.F.A. Vol 7 Jan 16		
War Diary	Meaulte	05/01/1916	29/01/1916
Heading	84th Bde. R.F.A. Vol 8		
War Diary	Meaulte	31/01/1916	29/02/1916
Heading	84 R F A Vol 9		
War Diary	Meaulte	01/03/1916	04/03/1916
War Diary	Daours	09/03/1916	20/03/1916
War Diary	Suzanne	31/03/1916	24/04/1916
War Diary	Maricourt	30/04/1916	31/05/1916
War Diary	Argoeuves	01/06/1916	11/06/1916

War Diary	Battle Quarters	11/06/1916	22/06/1916
War Diary	Billon Valley	11/06/1916	30/06/1916
Heading	18 Vol 13 84th Bde R.F.A. July 1916		
War Diary	Billon Valley	01/07/1916	01/07/1916
War Diary	Head Quarters	02/07/1916	02/07/1916
War Diary	Billon Valley	03/07/1916	08/07/1916
War Diary	Carnoy	09/07/1916	21/07/1916
War Diary	Bois De Tailles	22/07/1916	22/07/1916
War Diary	Argoeuves	23/07/1916	23/07/1916
War Diary	Erondelle	24/07/1916	27/07/1916
War Diary	Eecke	28/07/1916	01/08/1916
War Diary	La-Armee	02/08/1916	24/08/1916
War Diary	La-Mortier	25/08/1916	31/08/1916
War Diary	Brick-Fields (Albert)	01/09/1916	01/09/1916
War Diary	Usna Redoubt	02/09/1916	04/09/1916
War Diary	La Boiselle	05/09/1916	14/09/1916
War Diary	Contalmaison	15/09/1916	30/09/1916
Heading	War Diary For October 1916 84th Brigade R.F.A. Vol 16		
War Diary	Old Gun Pits 500 4de N W U S N A	01/10/1916	14/10/1916
War Diary	Donnet Post	15/10/1916	31/10/1916
Heading	War Diary For November 1916 84th Bde R.F.A. Vol 17		
War Diary	Donnets Post	01/11/1916	30/11/1916
Heading	War Diary of 84th Brigade R.F.A. from December 1st 1916 to December 31st 1916 (Volume VI)		
War Diary	Donnets Post	01/12/1916	02/12/1916
War Diary	Albert	03/12/1916	06/12/1916
War Diary	Grand-Laviers	07/12/1916	28/12/1916

WO 95/2025

16 Division
Divisional Troops
84 Brigade Royal Field Artillery

Jul 1915 - Dec 1916.

18TH DIVISION

84TH BDE R.F.A.
JLY 1915-DEC 1916

TO 4 ARMY

18 Div Arty

War Diary

84th Brigade R.F.A.

18th Division.

84th Brigade R.F.A.
Vol. I.
1-31-7-15
Dec 16

Army Form C. 2118.

WAR DIARY
or
INTELLIGENCE SUMMARY.
(Erase heading not required.)

Instructions regarding War Diaries and Intelligence Summaries are contained in F. S. Regs., Part II. and the Staff Manual respectively. Title pages will be prepared in manuscript.

Place	Date	Hour	Summary of Events and Information	Remarks and references to Appendices
OOST HOVE FARM	July 1	10 am	O.C. D/64 reported that an enemy machine gun had apparently been brought into position in the night in crater U.21.b.77 - It is hidden in the long grass in front of the German trenches and about 60 yards from our trenches	MAP Reference Sheet 28 / 20000 "B" Series NEUVE-EGLISE - MESSINES
			C/64 fired on enemy trenches South of the BIRDCAGE for registering	
			A/64 observing from AUGHEER CABARET U.27.b.77 fired on hostile trenches at U.22.c.45	
			B/64 did not fire but continued work on gun emplacements at U.25.a.57	
		7.0 pm	All quiet in front	
	2	8.15 am	D/64 fired at FACTORY FARM U.16.c.04 and at the trenches in the BIRDCAGE observing from GERMAN HOUSE in trench 31.	See Appendix VI for ZONES a night time
		11.30 am	C/64 fired at trenches South of the BIRDCAGE observing from ST YVES and from PALK VILLA U.21.d.56.	
			B/64 registered night lines U.22.C.H.7. observing from trench at ST YVES and also from trench 21	
		12.15 pm	C/64 fired on Enemy communication trench U.22.a.7.5. - corrector 126 3 pairs burst on target.	
		12.30 pm	Enemy 4.1 Howitzer shelled U.19.d.13. & U.25.a.89. but did not damage except to a telephone wire	See Appendix III for details of new position of...
		3.30 pm	D/64 fired on trench in BIRDCAGE observing from GERMAN HOUSE	
		5.0 pm	Enemy 4.1 Howitzer from direction of DEULEMONT fired a few shells into PLOEGSTEERT VILLAGE and on to HILL 63	
		7.0 pm	All quiet in front.	

Army Form C. 2118.

WAR DIARY
or
INTELLIGENCE SUMMARY.
(Erase heading not required.)

Place	Date	Hour	Summary of Events and Information	Remarks and references to Appendices
OOSTHOVE FARM	July 3	10-50 p.m (2.7.15)	Some rifle grenades were fired into trench 31 from the German trench opposite. On request of the Company Commander B/6th fired a round at the spot from which the grenades were thrown. The round effectually stopped any more grenades being fired.	
		10-20 a.m	D/6th Forward Observation Officer reported that the Germans had fired a few shell into wood behind trench 31. D/6th retaliated with shell fire on the BIRDCAGE. The German shells were apparently 4.1 Howitzer from direction of DEULEMONT - The O.C. B/6th observed from trap R8a together in German parapet at V.22.a.0.8. and a breach in parapet filled with planking. D/6th observing from St YVES V.15.d.1.5. fired on BIRDCAGE. The hot gun now explodes part of trench V.21.b.66. One shell burst along this trench & a flame 11-12 feet long was observed. Possibly something was ignited in the trenches. B/6th observing from trench at St YVES fired at end of Avenue V.22.c.8.7. and end of trench V.22.c.4.2. A/6th observing from AUGHEER CABARET registered LOOPHOLE FARM	
		7 p.m	All quiet in front.	
	4	6.25 a.m	The F.O.O. of C/6th observed German Aeroplane moving North East to S. West.	
		7-10 a.m	A German Field battery (probably 77 m.m. guns) in the direction of V.17.a WARNETON fired on our trenches 31.32 and St YVES. This battery fired about 150 shells altogether. The damage done was slight. At one time the battery was apparently searching trench 32, at another ranging on the newly	

WAR DIARY
or
INTELLIGENCE SUMMARY.

(Erase heading not required.)

Army Form C. 2118.

Place	Date	Hour	Summary of Events and Information	Remarks and references to Appendices
OOSTHOVE FARM	July 4		Visited Canadian Observation Post at ST YVES which may have been spotted by the aeroplane at 1-20 a.m.	
		8-10 a.m.	Another battery probably (4.1 howitzer) opened fire on our trench No 23 from the direction of DEULEMONT. About 50 shell burst in the tops of the trees in face of PLOEGSTEERT WOOD and in HUNTER'S AVENUE. Both H.E. & shrapnel were fired and the shelling continued on and off till about noon. At the request of the infantry C.B. & D. batteries retaliated. D/64 fired at the BIRDCAGE, C/64 at hostile trenches immediately S. of the BIRDCAGE & B/64 at enemy trench opposite to our trench 21, about V.22.C.2.7. This shelling of enemy trenches was successful in stopping the fire in the trenches. A/64 fired at LOOPHOLE FARM U.28.b.2.4.	
		5-25 p.m.	Enemy 4.1 Howitzer again fired about 20 rounds in vicinity of our trenches 20 & 21. The shell landed in trench 20. - No damage. D/6A has about completed work on new observation station at ST YVES	
		7-0 p.m.	All quiet in front	
	5		The O.C. B/64 has deduced the following formulae for using the 85 Fuze with the 80 fuze corrector scale - With barometer at 30 - " Add the constant 110 to the number of hundreds of yards in range. - This equals corrector reading. Example: Range 4200. 110 + 42 = Corrector 152. Range 2600. 110 + 26 = Corrector 136.	

Army Form C. 2118.

WAR DIARY
or
INTELLIGENCE SUMMARY.
(Erase heading not required.)

Instructions regarding War Diaries and Intelligence Summaries are contained in F. S. Regs., Part II. and the Staff Manual respectively. Title pages will be prepared in manuscript.

Place	Date	Hour	Summary of Events and Information	Remarks and references to Appendices
OOSTHOVE FARM	July 5		O.C. D/64 reports that one of our aeroplanes passed low over enemy trenches drawing rifle and machine gun fire. B/64 fired a few shrapnel which burst low over the trenches and this was successful in stopping the enemy's fire. From the evening statement of B/64 at ST YVES from trench 118 6 loopholes is plainly seen, one of them is being used by an enemy sniper with a telescope. From trench 118 6 loopholes in the Southern corner of the BIRDCAGE can also be plainly seen. The loopholes cut near of the loopholes in trench 118 reports that a gun from the loophole fired 3 rounds of shrapnel this afternoon at about 2.30 p.m. The shell passed over trench 118 & burst in PLOEGSTEERT WOOD. Snipers men would be plainly seen working at the loopholes at 7 p.m.	
	6		A/64 fired at German trenches U 28 A 45 and B/64 at support trench U 22 a 32. C/64 fired at trenches South of BIRDCAGE and B/64 a few rounds at spot in BIRDCAGE where shrews with scoops was seen. B/64 at 7 p.m. machine gun emplacement. The second bin of German trenches between U 18 2 0 and GRANDE HAIE FARM appears to have been strengthened with more barbed wire entanglements since yesterday. This morning a sniper was reported to have been knocked out by a sniper of the British from trench 118. The enemy sniper being near the loophole reported yesterday. C/64 registered PETITE HAIE FARM in U 23. A/64 shewing from R.U. CHEER CABARET fired at trench U 29 x 69 and U 22 a 51 with good effect. A German Aeroplane flew over ST YVES at 10.35 a.m. going west.	
"		6.30 p.m.	All quiet on front.	
	7	6 a.m.	A German aeroplane passed over ST YVES travelling from E to W.	
		10.30 a.m.	Enemy 77 m.m. field battery fired about 20 shell in vicinity of ST YVES. O.C. B/64 reports that a direct hit by shrapnel on	

Army Form C. 2118.

WAR DIARY
or
INTELLIGENCE SUMMARY.
(Erase heading not required.)

Instructions regarding War Diaries and Intelligence Summaries are contained in F. S. Regs., Part II. and the Staff Manual respectively. Title pages will be prepared in manuscript.

Place	Date	Hour	Summary of Events and Information	Remarks and references to Appendices
OOSTHOVE FARM	July	3 pm	On the brick wall of his observing station did no damage (STYVES)	
B 11 d 3 6			The company commander in trench 121 reported that 5 shell had fallen in his trench - 2/64 retaliated by firing on BIRDCAGE with good effect.	
Sheet 36 1/20000 (B Secn)		8 pm	Enemy 5·9 How shelled CHATEAU LA HUTTE from direction of DEULEMONT	
		8·30 pm	No 2 mountain battery & D/65 opened fire in BIRDCAGE - B/64 & D/64 fired on parapets exercises - no infantry at same time opened fire (rifle) from our trenches.	
		8·35 pm	B/64 C/64 & D/64 fired on BIRDCAGE with Shrapnel. From observing station at STYVES the shrapnel appeared to be well distributed over the enemy trenches in the BIRDCAGE. It was too dark to see effect at the time but later it would appear that damage to enemy trenches had been effected. New sand bags had been put up to fill gaps particularly at one place 50 yds north of BIRDCAGE. After our first burst of artillery fire the enemy opened with a considerable amount of machine gun fire. Enemy manned trenches south of LE GHEER - BASSEVILLE Rd & fired from two trenches 112 & 114. About 4 mm also Machine battery had rained the enemy guns shelled (77 mm & 4·2 How) PLOEGSTEERT WOOD. Trench were rauchet down by U·C. C/64 & D/64. Maj Lussey 72 mm being 1088, 4·1 1360, 4·2 1230. There would being positions of enemy batteries & about U 13 a - U 19 a - U 30 b - 2 trench mortars were also observed mag 137 which gave position at U 16 C 01.	
		12 midnight	The 35th Inf Bde reported that the Canadians in trench 121 might require assistance if one gues, as the Germans appeared to be manning same - D/64 & C/64 stood by but nothing further happened	
	8	4·30 am	Harassing officer of C/64 saw six Germans laying wire near U 22 C 07. They did dirt thin open and Enfield conto the enemy fire trench at U 14 C 01 appears to have several emplacements in it which may be used by trench mortars	
		10·30 am	C/64 observed a working party just E of BIRDCAGE, opened fire on it & scattered it. B/62 fired on enemy trench U 22 C 95 - of an artillery observing station	
			C/64 registered two rds on LE GHEER- WARNETON Rd U17 C96.	
		4·30	Enemy 4·1 How shelled CHATEAU LA HUTTE from direction of DEULEMONT	

1577 Wt. W10791/1773 500,000 1/15 D. D. & L. A.D.S.S./Forms/C. 2118.

Army Form C. 2118.

WAR DIARY
or
INTELLIGENCE SUMMARY.
(Erase heading not required.)

Instructions regarding War Diaries and Intelligence Summaries are contained in F.S. Regs., Part II. and the Staff Manual respectively. Title pages will be prepared in manuscript.

Place	Date	Hour	Summary of Events and Information	Remarks and references to Appendices
OOSTHOVE FARM	July 9	5 p.m.	A good deal of movement was noticed today of Enemy Trenches in BIRDCAGE. A canvas screen has been put up plainly seen from C/62 observation station at ST YVES. Then was seen crossing from communication trench of fire trench at about 5.15 – possibly a relief. C/62 opened fire on it & by the sand bags close to the screen were damaged fire must have been effective.	
			Observing officer of B/62 reports a second dug out having been made in the night in German 3rd line trench at V.22.a.92. The men our reported yesterday being at J.22.a.89 – both lost little observation posts. The camouflage screen & wooden excavation of C/62 and about 6pm men partly camouflaged were seen going behind it. C/62 opened fire & no movement has been seen there since –	
			Enemy shelled (4.1) from direction of DEULEMONT B.17 & 25 about 200 x South east of OOSTHOVE FARM. All batteries notice that registrations made in day time are noticeable at night & that than 50 & 100 yards has to be added for night firing at 3000 yds and under.	
		9 p.m.	Canadians exploded a mine opposite trench 121 which caused a certain amount of rifle & machine gun fire from both sides. Enemy 77mm battery fired 6 rounds which fell in rear of trench 123 – approximate position of battery being B.17.A.	
		10.30 p.m.	Enemy M.G. How from DEULEMONT direction fired some shell into LE GHEER & PLOEGSTEERT WOOD	
		11 p.m.	Two Austrian battery opened fire on WARNETON ROAD and in retaliation enemy 77mm battery fired some shell into V.27 & B.6. Some of these rounds hit Q/62 observation station & the some damage – Machine of enemy is some have observed by D.C. Q/62. 12.30 mag from AU GHEER CABARET.	
	10	6 a.m.	Observing officer C/62 noticed movement of a sluice U.22.2.6. Enemy infantry in what appeared to be a Mackin- to fired 10 rounds with good effect on this place and communication trench behind C/62 reports enemy fire trench V.18.c.01 has had a lot of work expended on it again – new sand bags put up with and a new loop hole in parapet unknown.	

1577 Wt. W10791/1773 500,000 1/15 D. D. & L. A.D.S.S./Forms/C. 2118.

Army Form C. 2118.

WAR DIARY
or
INTELLIGENCE SUMMARY.

(Erase heading not required.)

Instructions regarding War Diaries and Intelligence Summaries are contained in F. S. Regs., Part II. and the Staff Manual respectively. Title pages will be prepared in manuscript.

Place	Date	Hour	Summary of Events and Information	Remarks and references to Appendices
OOSTHOVE FARM	July 10	9.30 a.m	D/164 fired 10 rounds at troops seen along track between FACTORY FARM and BIRDCAGE. They were hit a sand bags displaced at intervals during the day. Enemy shelled PLOEGSTEERT VILLAGE & # W & S. 9th C/64 a B 12 b.	Very heavy
	11	2.15 a.m	The Canadians called for assistance of the 63rd Bty. fire & heavy rifle & machine gun fire was opened from our trenches. The enemy did not respond & all remained quiet. D/164 opened C/64 during the day fired at the enemy previously referred to, when a good many men who were passing some in khaki & others in blue grey uniform. Some damage was done to parapet & the many houses near & spots when passing this spot. C/64 obtained a direct hit on PETITE MAIE FARM. A new emplacement is seen being made by the 7th in a distance of 50 yards D18c01. D/164 noticed some digging being done near FACTORY FARM U.6.c.0.3. The enemy shelled PLOEGSTEERT village & ST YVES and at 5 P.m. a shell wounded Lieut. Corries B.2.A Bde a 2 O/164 in a trench at edge of PLOEGSTEERT Wood (Lieut Corries was slightly wounded).	
		12.50 p.m 3.15		
	12		At 10.50 p.m on the 11th C/164 at Poletsing Road U.15.b.35— heard transport moving on WARNETON PONT ROUGE road appeared to be about the road junction S. of LA BASSEVILLE at U.17.c.a.o. They fired 2 rounds gun fire at the point. The transport halted. At 11.0 P.m when it moved again another round gun fire was brought to bear. The movement noticed by C/164 man has seen & 5 men were seen carrying planks. B.C. C/64 visited trenches U.15.b.20 & found much the improvement. The Canadians reported much movement in BIRDCAGE, probably a relief going on. D/64 fired 2 rounds gun fire & obtained good low bursts just over their trenches in the BIRDCAGE a/64 shelled enemy trenches at V.22 C & 2 and knocked a hole in their parapet.	
		7 a.m		
	13	11.30 am	Enemy shelled PLOEGSTEERT village, and again in the afternoon — a telephonist 7 S.A. Bde was wounded (all slightly) Enemy probably heard transport going to infantry & making a great noise in a very 6 ZAN Bde. from a shell hole	

1577 Wt. W10791/1773 500,000 1/15 D. D. & L. A.D.S.S./Forms/C. 2118.

Army Form C. 2118.

Instructions regarding War Diaries and Intelligence Summaries are contained in F.S. Regs., Part II. and the Staff Manual respectively. Title pages will be prepared in manuscript.

WAR DIARY
or
INTELLIGENCE SUMMARY.
(Erase heading not required.)

Place	Date	Hour	Summary of Events and Information	Remarks and references to Appendices
OOST HOVE FARM	14.		Magpie leaving was 1090 this would bring the batteries (15cm How) position of #8 about 1400 yards south of the O in DEULEMONT	
			C/84 fired some rounds at a house in DEULEMONT from which a man was seen throwing from a window. At 9 p.m. last night the Canadians fired a mine opposite trench 121. The explosion was followed by heavy rifle & machine gun fire from both sides. Enemy artillery fo-th with ours — the Batteries # 837, 3H stood by. The crater appeared about half way between our & the German trenches but at the front of trench 121 it cost our own parapet. It would appear that the Enemy SOS signal is changed daily — on the 7th inst when the BIRDCAGE was disturbed 1 red & 2 green rockets were fired — last night 3 red were fired.	
		12 noon	B/84 fired at loophole opposite our trench 122 & also at house at U22 c.3.4. which may be an observation station.	
		3.40 pm	Enemy shelled PLOEGSTEERT — LE GHEER ROAD with 4.1 Howitzers. 6 shells fell well in front of C/84 battery position & 7 in PLOEGSTEERT village. OC C/84 saw offices in grey overcoats near the screen — they appeared to be discussing something in the direction of our O.S. & to be taking angles.	
	15		C/84 can now observe a part of the main road WARNETON — LILLE — movements of mounted men & cyclists can be seen. A careful watch will be kept on this road and on the railway near it. 2 men on iron rod past the Suere.	
		9.0 a.m	Trench 120 was shelled by trench mortars	
		3.40 pm	Enemy shelled trench 121 4.1 Howitzers. The zone of the brigade has been extended & the 12th Division now forms part of the 2nd corps *	* see Appendix IV
			A/84 registered night lines from WARNAVE BROOK to LE GHEER — BASSEVILLE ROAD and fired a few rounds at LOOPHOLE FARM U.22.D.3.4.	
		6.30 pm	Enemy shelled NEUVE EGLISE and succeeded in demolishing church spire and setting the church on fire	

Army Form C. 2118.

WAR DIARY
or
INTELLIGENCE SUMMARY.
(Erase heading not required.)

Instructions regarding War Diaries and Intelligence Summaries are contained in F. S. Regs., Part II and the Staff Manual respectively. Title pages will be prepared in manuscript.

Place	Date	Hour	Summary of Events and Information	Remarks and references to Appendices
OOSTHOVE FARM	July 15	6.pm	B/64 fired 10 shells at loopholes in parapet 100 yards south of FACTORY FARM U.18.c.0.3. Also lobbed in very conspicuous and may be a machine gun emplacement. Part of the parapet was destroyed and the gap swept by Canadian machine gun. The Bosche has been repaired.	
	16	4-30 a.m.	Three men seen carrying long planks from the screen in the BIRDCAGE.	
		11-12	Enemy 77 m.m. battery from direction of BASSEVILLE fired about 14 shells at our trenches at ST YVES. Some damage done in the wiring of shrapnel sandbags. After the shelling ceased a German officer came from behind the screen and looked from some time at ST YVES.	
		3-10	Enemy 4.1 Howitzer fired some shell at trench 121 and two into PLOEGSTEERT VILLAGE. Some activity today was observed in BIRDCAGE, many periscopes and a few sniper's rifles.	
	17		Last night B/64 moved to a new position taking over the position of C/63. from 2am a Observation station etc see appendix IV A/64 have observed a grey shed with black sandbags at the bottom of it. Our infantry state that a machine gun fired from there last night. A/64 also report a trench running parallel to German trench and about 30 yards behind it this is opposite to own 111-112 trenches. Fresh earth has been thrown up in this communication trench showing from U.22.A.4.0. towards LOG HOLT FARM.	
		5pm	C/64 reports the presence of a small black dog in parapet of BIRDCAGE otherwise all quiet.	
	18		A very quiet day - Enemy fired at trench 130 at 10.40 am and 12 noon shells fell in PLOEGSTEERT WOOD C/64 fired at barricade on LE BIZET road U.22.c.3.4 also at cottage U.22.C.8.5 - D/64 fired 12 rounds searching the road and railway near PETITE HALE FARM U.23 central where mounted staff were seen. 2/64 reports movement on the DEULEMONT road near LES ECLUSES U.30A - B/64 bombarded regd. bosches of the new zones.	

LES ECLUSES U.30A - B/64 bombarded A.D.S.S./Forms/C. 2118.
1577 Wt.W10791/1773 500,000 1/15 D. D. & L.

Army Form C. 2118.

WAR DIARY
or
INTELLIGENCE SUMMARY.
(Erase heading not required).

Instructions regarding War Diaries and Intelligence Summaries are contained in F. S. Regs., Part II. and the Staff Manual respectively. Title pages will be prepared in manuscript.

Place	Date	Hour	Summary of Events and Information	Remarks and references to Appendices
BOSTHOVE FARM	July 19	4.30 a.m.	German aeroplane was fired at by our anti aircraft guns. It had flown over the position of C/64 and at 5-30 a.m. another was seen with black crosses on each wing. Also at 6-55 a.m. another was seen with black crosses on the wings.	
			B/64 continued registration of 166 roms - D/64 fired on enemy trench opposite to our 129 - C/64 fired at some men at LES ECLUSES U30A and at enemy trench U16C4.	
		6.0 p.m.	Germans in trench opposite 18D (Appx D) displayed a board with "we are going to attack at 7 o'clock without".	
		7.30 p.m.	All quiet.	
	20		Continued from last night. D/64 observed parties of men who had been bathing in the LYS - they shelled them also the cottage into which they went (U30d 107). These men were wearing dark blue uniforms with neckwear caps. Others were seen on Road (U30d.55) in helmets and lighter coloured uniforms. D/64 also fired on transport (U30d.107). This fire believed to be effective.	
			B/64 at request of Infantry fired at working party opposite trench 103 and dispersed it. B/64 sources news from LONDON FARM.	
			C/64 fired at TILLEUL [U11c54] for registration purposes.	
		5 a.m.	Enemy Howitzer shelled PLOEGSTEERT WOOD and at 8-30 vicinity of PLOEGSTEERT village.	
		11 a.m.	D/64 shelled and dispersed working party in garden U.30.d.10.7.	
		11.30 "	A/64 shelled LOOPHOLE FARM U.26.b.3.5. & communication trench	
		12.30 p.m.	Enemy 4.1 (How) from direction of LES ECLUSES fired 6 rounds close to THE CONVENT at LE GHEER. No damage done.	
			B/64 fired at BLANCHISSERIE C.S.C.6.6.	

Army Form C. 2118.

WAR DIARY
or
INTELLIGENCE SUMMARY.
(Erase heading not required.)

Place	Date	Hour	Summary of Events and Information	Remarks and references to Appendices
DOGTHOVE FARM	July 20	4.37pm	D/64 and C/64 each fired one round for Test S.O.S. on their night lines.	
		4.45pm	Several parties were observed by C/64 in road near LES ECLUSES O.30.c. They were fired on and dispersed. D/64 observed two electric cables in trench opposite our 121 leading to the Lys, and shelled this place with effect.	
	21	at 10.25	last night all batteries received "TEST S.O.S." & fired one round. Enemy fired 6 shells at trenches 106 & 107 in apparently retaliation. A/64 is of opinion that these shell were fired by enemy 77 m.m. battery situated about U29.c.5.8.	
		3.15	German aeroplane flew over ST YVES going West. C/64 shelled a working party at GANGERS HUT U28.C.5.7.	
		6.15	Enemy 4.1 & 5.9 (How) shelled PLOEGSTEERT village apparently in retaliation for our Howitzer shelling DEULEMONT. The fire was much more rapid than usual 4 shell coming at a time. Some damage done to roadway & houses.	
		5.50pm	C/64 fired on working party in trench U23.c.B.6. This battery also fired at PETITE MUNE FARM (U.23. central) four rounds were fired one of which was a direct hit.	
	22	9.4am	Transport was seen in road U.20.b.23. going towards the Lys. bad light made observation difficult. B/64 & C/64 fired at LES ECLUSES. E/64 on road & B/64 on a chimney U22.a.99.	
	23.	6.10 to 6.30pm	Enemy shelled cross roads in PLOEGSTEERT & the PLOEGSTEERT - ARMENTIERES road with S.O.(H.E.). At same time enemy 77 m.m. fired shrapnel East and S.E. of PLOEGSTEERT - D/64 reported a new embrasure in enemy front line trench and fired on it on the 22nd. which new barbed wire is also found by front line & second line trench U21.b.99. north of BIRDCAGE.	

Army Form C. 2118.

WAR DIARY
or
INTELLIGENCE SUMMARY.
(Erase heading not required.)

Instructions regarding War Diaries and Intelligence Summaries are contained in F. S. Regs., Part II. and the Staff Manual respectively. Title pages will be prepared in manuscript.

Place	Date	Hour	Summary of Events and Information	Remarks and references to Appendices
OOSTHOVE FARM Bn H.Q.	July 23	At 7.15 p.m.	At 7.15 p.m. 22nd C/64 fired at a working party strengthening a trench not previously observed running from about U.22.a.8.5. to U.18.2.5.A. They dispersed at first round. Trench not deep so they could still be seen and shrapnel would appear to be effective.	
		10.30 to 12 noon	Enemy 77mm battery from direction of PONT ROUGE opened fire between PLOEGSTEERT village and position of A/64. All the shrapnel burst very high. Shortly after several 4.1 (How) from direction of WARNETON also opened a gradually increasing their range till they got to OOSTHOVE FARM they put about 18 shell around the farm getting 2 direct hits on the farm buildings. In retaliation A/64 shelled LOOPHOLE FARM and B/64 LONG BARN U.28.d.1.5. A/64 got 3 direct hits on buildings. B/64 also shelled enemy front line trench. B/64 also fired on and dispersed a working party in trench opposite trench 103. B/64 near observed farm LONDON FARM C.3.2.5.8.	
		8 pm	all quiet	
	24		A party of Germans in grey capes were dispersed by C/64 last night on the road near LES ECLUSES.	
		8.15 & 9 am	Enemy 77mm & 4.1 (how) fired a few rounds at PLOEGSTEERT. Then lengthening their range fired a few rounds at OOSTHOVE FARM. They then lengthened again & shelled the outskirts of NIEPPE. The shrapnel burst high & the H.E. HE nearly all burst on percussion. B/64 noticed Germans x 2 and 3 passing a gap in their front line parapet & firing into a kind in front of it. This is opposite trench 103. When working party was seen yesterday a fire upon by D/64. D/64 fired at LES ECLUSES & D/64 as well as C/64 registered TULLUZ U.10.C.	
		4.10 pm	Enemy fired two rounds 4.1 into PLOEGSTEERT VILLAGE by D.E. no 4 Battery 1st & 8th Canadian Art. from HILL 63. This fire was observed	

Army Form C. 2118.

WAR DIARY
or
INTELLIGENCE SUMMARY.
(Erase heading not required.)

Instructions regarding War Diaries and Intelligence Summaries are contained in F. S. Regs, Part II. and the Staff Manual respectively. Title pages will be prepared in manuscript.

Place	Date	Hour	Summary of Events and Information	Remarks and references to Appendices
OOSTHOVE FARM	July 25		At 6.15 last night B/64 fired at a party apparently working on a trench in front of their own front trench & behind their wire.	
		7.0 pm	B/64 shelled a platoon on the road near LES ECLUSES. One platoon of about 40 men each were observed & one platoon scattered & took refuge. Later 3 transport wagons brought up to space these spots at a gallop.	
		9.40 to 10.10 pm	Enemy shelled Canadian trenches and HYDE PARK CORNER.	
			B/64 from LONDON FARM reports an embrasure with a "steel shield and loophole with slide" on enemy front trench opposite trench 103. B/64 fired at it with shrapnel & registered the place. Work still goes on at enemy trench reported yesterday. Men seen wearing a "shade of khaki" similar to ours - Seven with round caps, dark with white bands, others with khaki caps and red bands. Men are seen at work & wire fixed on here with effect. B/64 received that S.O.S. last night & fired - e/64 fired at LOOPHOLE FARM. A good deal of movement noticed seen in BIRDCAGE. They appear to be deepening their trenches	
	26		B/64 reports a lot of movement on road near LES ECLUSES. U.S.a.d.10.8. Officer on horseback are seen going to & coming from their houses - Movements point to a Headquarters being in one of these houses. Attack made by our howitzers in BEULEMONT CHURCH SPIRE has been repaired with wood. Several German Aeroplanes passed over position of c/64 between 5 & 7 pm last night.	
		11-30am	B/64 shelled bridge at U.30a.5.9 and U.30 b.25	
		2.30	Infantry in trench 116 were being much worried by rifle grenades from near the Barricade on LECHEER ROAD. C/64 fired 8 rounds shrapnel at this point and silenced the grenadiers.	

1577 Wt. W10791/1773 500,000 1/15 D. D. & L. A.D.S.S./Forms/C. 2118.

Army Form C. 2118.

WAR DIARY
or
INTELLIGENCE SUMMARY.
(Erase heading not required.)

Instructions regarding War Diaries and Intelligence Summaries are contained in F. S. Regs., Part II. and the Staff Manual respectively. Title pages will be prepared in manuscript.

Place	Date	Hour	Summary of Events and Information	Remarks and references to Appendices
OOSTHOVE FARM	26	5.25	A/64 fired at LONGBARN U22 d 67 when a German was seen observing. Missed several direct hits on the observer left the place.	
			B/64 fired at the Steel plate opposite trench 103. Several direct hits were obtained. H.E. would be useful at this spot.	
			D/64 shelled bridge at U17A 84. U30 a 89. U30 b 25. also Arnicé and garden at LES ECLUSES	
	27	5.30 am	Bott C & D/64 dispersed working parties at U22 a 55 & U23 a 29. Also fire at and registered houses and road at PONT ROUGE.	
			Enemy H.1 (how) shelled the neighbourhood of ST YVES & at 2-30 they shelled PLOEGSTEERT VILLAGE	
		5.30 pm	C/64 fired at PETITE HAIE FARM & obtained several direct hits. also swept railway & road where much movement had been lately. Line is being cut near LES ECLUSES by civilians	
		7.45	Enemy again shelled PLOEGSTEERT VILLAGE and H.Co. of 5/64. Corpl STARMER was wounded severely. He subsequently died of wounds on 28th	
	28	7 am	Hostile working parts, about 15 men was seen moving along newly dug shallow trench from U22 A55 & U23C79 they were carrying tools & appeared to be knocking off work.	
			B/64 reports digging at various points opposite our trenches 102 & 103. The sap opposite 103 is now deep enough to hide men up to their shoulders. Communication trenches in rear are also being improved. At	
		7.30	B/64 fired into this sap with effect & into the main trench near the Steel plate.	
			Enemy guns have not fired today.	
	29		Our Infantry in trenches 115, 116, 117 report that they are continually being sniped at from a row of trees U23a75. B/64 shelled this spot at 4 am today. Since when the snipers have not been active. As reported a lot of work has been going on at trenches opposite 103 - trenches being improved. no work	

1577 Wt.W10791/1773 500,000 1/15 D. D. & L. A.D.S.S./Forms/C. 2118.

Army Form C. 2118.

WAR DIARY
or
INTELLIGENCE SUMMARY.
(Erase heading not required.)

Instructions regarding War Diaries and Intelligence Summaries are contained in F. S. Regs., Part II. and the Staff Manual respectively. Title pages will be prepared in manuscript.

Place	Date	Hour	Summary of Events and Information	Remarks and references to Appendices
DOST HOVE FARM	29		Seen from to-day	
			C/64 observed a working party behind the barricade in LE GHEER ROAD	
		1.40 pm	Enemy A1 (new) shelled PLOEGSTEERT WOOD from direction of DEULEMONT and again from 3.20 & 4.15	
		6 p.m.	C/64 noticed a number of Germans in green-grey forage caps passing a gap in enemy front line trench north of BIRDCAGE U.21.b.9.8. An officer wearing same coloured cap & red band with gold braid in rear crossed this gap 3 times in 5 minutes	
	30	11-30 a.m.	C/64 fired at PETITE HAIE FARM where movement was observed - fire appeared to be effective. More earth has been thrown up in front of German front trench opposite.	
		2 p.m.	B/64 fired at the portion of enemy trench opposite the centre of our trench 102. This produced a retaliation from enemy 77mm field battery from direction of PONT ROUGE on to our trenches 103 & 104. Their shell fell over our front line trenches	
		5 p.m.	Enemy Field guns shelled our trench 122. One H.E. shell made a hit in the parapet. 8/64 fired at German front line trench just north of the BIRDCAGE then lifted on to the road between the GANGERS COTTAGE & DEULEMONT U.22 A.12. When movement was observed.	
31	5-45 a.m.	D/64 shelled enemy trenches and loopholes opposite trench 122 also the road behind GANGER'S COTTAGE U.23.d.12. and Heindly House U.22.d.00. Near the latter movement was visible - there has been no further movement observed on road near LES ECLUSES by day since 8/64 shelled the infantry there	
		6.45 a.m.	A working party was seen and fired at at U.21.k.9.3. Half an hour later it was again seen & a salvo fired which appeared to be effective	

Army Form C. 2118.

WAR DIARY
or
INTELLIGENCE SUMMARY.
(Erase heading not required.)

Instructions regarding War Diaries and Intelligence Summaries are contained in F. S. Regs., Part II. and the Staff Manual respectively. Title pages will be prepared in manuscript.

Place	Date	Hour	Summary of Events and Information	Remarks and references to Appendices
COST HOVE FARM	July 31	6 a.m.	Enemy 4.1 howitzer shelled our trenches 118 & 117. C/64 fired at enemy trenches opposite in retaliation at request of our Infantry. Eight rounds were fired apparently with good effect. Enemy Howitzer ceased firing.	
		8 a.m.	German aeroplane was shewed by C/64 flying west.	
		6.30 p.m.	A/64 and B/64 shelled Enemy Support and communication trenches in V.28.d. and C.4.b. firing in conjunction with the 63rd and 65th Brigades R.F.A. She shrapnel fire appeared to be well distributed over the allotted zone and most of the shell burst low right over the Enemy communication trenches. Enemy retaliated with 77 m.m & 4.1 Howitzer on to our trenches - LEGHEER, the gun positions of B/64 and B/63 and LE BIZET, and over PLOEGSTEERT. C/64 again retaliated by firing on to DEOLEMONT - and A/64 by firing on LOOPHOLE FARM.	

R.W.Duff Capt. R.F.A.

ADJUTANT 34TH BDE. R. FIELD ARTY

Identification Trace for use with Artillery Maps.

Appendix II

Tracing taken from Sheet 28 SW + 36 NW
of the 1:20000 map of Belgium + France

Signature .... Date ....

Army Form C. 2118.

WAR DIARY
or
INTELLIGENCE SUMMARY.
(Erase heading not required.)

Place	Date	Hour	Summary of Events and Information	Remarks and references to Appendices
OOST HOVE FARM			Appendix III	
			At the end of June the 48th South Midland Field Artillery Brigade (Territorial) to which division we had been attached	
			Moved away & the 12th Div was made part of the 3rd Corps under General Pulteney. This Corps consist of Canadians, 12th Div, 27th Div and 5th Div. The 12th Div has on its right the Canadian Div. The 64th Bde. R.F.A. is on the left of the 12th Div having on its immediate right the 63rd Bde. R.F.A. and the Canadians on its immediate left.	MAP references BELGIUM & FRANCE B Series Sheet 28. and " 3.6
			The 65th Brigade (Howitzer) have a battery supporting each F.A. Brigade & covering the front of these Brigades. The 64th Bde zone is covered by D/65 (Major BALSTON).	
			The trenches in the zone of the 64th Bde R.A. are occupied by the 35th, 36th & 37th Infantry brigades (12th Division) under Br Gen Straubenzee - Br Gen Bonnersets. Bonneridale & Br Gen Fowler (The whole 12th Div being commanded by Major Gen Wing-)	
			The trenches have been reconnoitred. The zone of 64th brigade includes trench 115 to 120 inclusive.	
			The right flank of 64th batteries are in enemy front line trenches opposite the trenches covered by our own right	
			lines, viz A/64 covers trench 115	Battery position C.1.a.2.7
			B/64 " " 116	" " U.27.b.77
			C/64 " " 117-8-9.	" " U.15.a.2.5
			D/64 " " 12.0	" " U.25.d.5.7
			The observation stations by day are as follows	
			A/64 —— AU GHEER CABARET	U.27.b.77
			B/64 —— St YVES (bunch)	U.15.a.2.5
			C/64 —— St YVES near POST OFFICE	U.15.d.5
			D/64 —— St YVES	U.15.a.1.5 U.25.b.3.2 U.19.e.1.2

Army Form C. 2118.

WAR DIARY
or
INTELLIGENCE SUMMARY.
(Erase heading not required.)

Place	Date	Hour	Summary of Events and Information	Remarks and references to Appendices
			Appendix III continued	
			Communication by day. Each Observation Station is in telephone communication with its battery and RIFLE HOUSE in PLOEGSTEERT WOOD.	
			by night Telephonist in trenches with company commanders are in direct communication with their batteries and RIFLE HOUSE.	
			RIFLE HOUSE is the head quarters of the battalion manning the trenches covered by our guns but has an officer and a telephonist at RIFLE HOUSE all day and night also a telephonist from each battery & Bn. H.Q.	
			Brigade H.Q. is in direct communication with all batteries and RIFLE HOUSE on separate wires.	
			Brigade H.Q. for want of a better place are rather too far back & this has entailed a large amount of telephone wire having to be put up. Duplication of batteries & single wire to RIFLE HOUSE making in all 22 miles. This is however quite apart from battery wires to their Observation Stations, trenches & RIFLE HOUSE.	
			6th B. Brigade Am. Col. is at its old position B-19 B.14.C.10.5. Supplies S.A.A. to 37th Inf. Bde. whether in reserve or in the trenches.	

WAR DIARY
or
INTELLIGENCE SUMMARY.

Army Form C. 2118.

Place	Date	Hour	Summary of Events and Information	Remarks and references to Appendices
			Appendix 4	
			About the 15th of this month (July) the 12th Division was made part of the 2nd Corps under Gen. Ferguson. The fate of the Division are the 50th (Territorials) the 28th and the Canadians. The Canadians are on our immediate left & the BN 84 is on the left of the 12th Div. The B/84 R.A. is now distributed & the 35th Infantry Brigade under Brig. Gen Shambrizie - our Zone was extended southwards & is now over the trenches occupied by two Battalions. Their H.Q are at "Rifle House" and "Reserve Farm". The 35th Inf Brigade HQ being at "Support Farm". The Brigade Am Col (84th R.F.A.) now supplies the 35th Inf Brigade with S.A.A.	See appendix IV
			Regoate showing Zones covered by batteries	

Trench	Battalion	Battery	Zone
102, 103, 104, 105	Essex or Suffolk regt H.Q. Reserve Fm	B/84	Cross Roads C.4.a MODLIN DE LA RABEQUE FARM to WARNAVE BROOK (both inclusive)
106, 107, 108, 110, 111, 112	do	A/64	WARNAVE BROOK (exclusive) to LEGHEER - LA BASSEVILLE Road exclusive
113, 114, 115	Berks or Hants regt H.Q. RIFLE Ho	C/64	LEGHEER - LA BASSEVILLE Road to PATHWAY U.22.a.4.1 (both inclusive)
119, 120	do	D/64	PATHWAY exclusive to South of BIRDCAGE

Observation Stations by day

B/64 "OBSERVATION FARM" close to RESERVE FARM
A/64 AUGHEER CABARET
C/64 St YVES
D/64 St YVES and GERMAN HOUSE

	Communication by night	7.30 pm to 7.30 am
B/64	with own telephonist with company Co. in trenches	
A/64		110
C/64		116
D/64		120

One officer from A & B batteries alternately and one telephonist from each of the two batteries is on duty at OBSERVATION FARM (close to RESERVE FARM)
and one officer from C & D batteries alternately and one telephonist from each of the two batteries is on duty at RIFLE HOUSE

N.B. D/65 (How) covers own zone as before

Identification Trace for use with Artillery Maps.

Appendix. 5.

			8	9	10	11 WARNETON	12
			14	15	16	17	18
		19	20	21	22	23	24
		25	26	27	28	29	30
			Ploegsteert	Vernes			
5	6	1	2	3	4	5	6
11	12	7	8	9	10	11 Frelinghien	12

Tracing taken from Sheet 28 SW. & 36 NW.

of the 1: 20,000 map of Belgium & France.

Signature .... Date ....

121/6607

18th Division

84th Brigade R.F.A.

Vol: II.

From 31 July to 31 Aug 15

WAR DIARY
or
INTELLIGENCE SUMMARY

(Erase heading not required.)

Army Form C. 2118

H.Q. 84 Bde R.F.A.

Place	Date 1915	Hour	Summary of Events and Information	Remarks and references to Appendices
COISY	July 31.	—	In Frionae.	
"	Aug 1	—	"	
HEILLY	2	3.pm	Arrived by route march with Brigade complete	
"	3	—	In Frionae.	
BRAY	4	12mn	Arrived BRONFAY FARM, 2m N.E. of BRAY with "B" & "C" Batteries. 84 Bde R.F.A. > 5th Division. Was attached to 8th Bde R.F.A. relieving French Batteries.	
"	5	—	Commenced relief of French Batteries.	
"	6	—	Continued relief; registered targets	

C. E. English
Col.
O/g 84 Bde R.F.A.

WAR DIARY
or
INTELLIGENCE SUMMARY

(Erase heading not required.)

Army Form C. 2118

H.Q. 82 Bde. R.F.A.

Place	Date	Hour	Summary of Events and Information	Remarks and references to Appendices
BRONFAY	1915 8.viii	9 a.m.	Observation station (1500x N by E of bivouac) spasmodically shelled: about 6 rounds: no result.	
	9.viii		Nil	
	10 "		Nil	
	11 "		Nil	
	12 "		Nil	
	13 "		Nil	
	14 "		BRONFAY FARM slightly shelled (300x N by W of bivouac) 1 man (R.E.) killed.	

C. Enright
Col.
Cdg. 82 Bde. R.F.A.

WAR DIARY
or
INTELLIGENCE SUMMARY

(Erase heading not required.)

H.Q. 84 Bde R.F.A.

Army Form C. 21.

Place	Date	Hour	Summary of Events and Information	Remarks and references to Appendices
BRONFAY FARM (near BRAY)	15 to 21 Aug	10/15	Nil.	
BRONFAY FARM	22.viii		6 rounds fired at road crossing, BRAY, in prolongation of wagon lines of B/84 and H.Q/64. 3 horses hit, 1 seriously, subsequently shot.	
	23.viii		Nil.	
MEAULTE	24.25 viii 12 n		Handed over command of Centre Group 5th Div. and took over left Group 18 Div. ("Q": R.H.A., C/82, A/64, B/64, C/64, B/84, C/55.)	
	26.viii		Nil	
	27.viii		"	
	28.viii		"	
	29.viii		"	
	30.viii		"	
	31.viii		"	

C. Englich Col.
O/o 84 Bde. R.F.A.

31.8.16.

121/6802

18th Division

84th Bde. RFA. Amm: Col:

Vol: I

August 15.

WAR DIARY
or
INTELLIGENCE SUMMARY

(Erase heading not required.)

Army Form C. 2118

Instructions regarding War Diaries and Intelligence Summaries are contained in F.S. Regs, Part II. and the Staff Manual respectively. Title Pages will be prepared in manuscript.

8th BRIGADE R.F.A.
Reg. No. 11
Date 31-8-16
AMMUNITION COLUMN

Place	Date	Hour	Summary of Events and Information	Remarks and references to Appendices
BETSY	1.8.15	—	nothing to report	
HEILLY	2	10 a.m.	marched to HEILLY	
"	3		nothing to report	
"	4		"	
ETINEHEM	5	10 a.m.	marched to ETINEHEM and become attached to 8th Division	
"	6		nothing to report	
"	7		"	
"	8		"	
"	9		"	
"	10		"	
"	11		"	
"	12		"	
"	13		"	
"	14		"	
"	15		"	
"	16		"	
"	17		"	
"	18		"	
"	19		"	
"	20		"	
"	21		"	
"	22		"	
"	23		"	
"	24		"	
TREUX	25	8.30 p.m.	marched to TREUX	
"	26		nothing to report	to rejoin 18th Division	
"	27		"	
"	28		"	
"	29		"	
"	30		"	
"	31		"	

J. Constable Captain, R.F.A.,
Comdg. Ammn. Col. 8th Bde. R.F.A.

Army Form C. 2118

WAR DIARY
or
INTELLIGENCE SUMMARY

18th DIVISION

(Erase heading not required.)

Instructions regarding War Diaries and Intelligence Summaries are contained in F.S. Regs., Part II. and the Staff Manual respectively. Title Pages will be prepared in manuscript.

Place	Date	Hour	Summary of Events and Information	Remarks and references to Appendices

SOUTHAMPTON.	26th.	5.30 a.m.	Embarked at Southampton strength
			
			OFFICERS. ANIMALS.
			Capt. R.P. Constable, 1. Horses including 4 attached 42.
			2/Lt. J. P. Phillips, 1. A.S.C.
			" W. T. Boston, 1. Mules, 154.
			" S. R. Gibbon, 1.
			Other ranks including 196.
			2 A.S.C. drivers attached. 151.
			                        155.
				VEHICLES.
				Ammn. Wagons, 16.
				L.G.S. " 8.
				G.S. " 8.
				G.S. "(Attached) 2.
				Water cart, 1.
				Bicycle, 1.
				         36.

HARVE.	27th.	9 a.m.	Arrived at HARVE entrained at 11.0 p.m. for destination unknown.	
LONGUEAU	28th	1.30pm	Arrived at LONGUEAU and marched to COISY a village about 9 miles North East of AMIENS.	
COISY.	29th.		Nothing to report.	
"	30th.		" " "	
"	31st.		" " "	

sd. R. Constable, Captain, R.F.A.
Commanding Ammunition Column 84th. Bde., RFA

121/6607

18th Division

"A"/84 Battery R.F.A.
Vol.: I
From 20 July to 5 Aug 15

Army Form C. 2118

A/84 RFA

WAR DIARY
or
INTELLIGENCE SUMMARY
(Erase heading not required.)

Instructions regarding War Diaries and Intelligence Summaries are contained in F. S. Regs., Part II. and the Staff Manual respectively. Title Pages will be prepared in manuscript.

Place	Date 1915	Hour	Summary of Events and Information	Remarks and references to Appendices
HEYTESBURY	July 20		Battery placed on War footing	BEF
WARMINSTER	26		Entrained 2 officers 70 men of Right X at 11.25 am & 2 officers 65 men at 12.55 pm	BEF BEF
			Embarked at Southampton 35 men & 2 officers on MONA QUEEN 102 - " - 2 " - S.W. Miller	BEF
HARVE	27	5 pm	Disembarked & proceeded to Rest Camp No 5	BEF BEF
-	28	10.39 pm	Entrained at Point 4 for Amiens	BEF
-	28	11.30 pm	Detrained	BEF
AMIENS	29	2.30 am	Arrived at Camp & took up billets	BEF
COISY	30		In billets	BEF
-	31		"	BEF

B.A. Browne Capt. RFA
OC A/84 RFA

WAR DIARY or INTELLIGENCE SUMMARY

Army Form C. 2118

A/84 RFA

Place	Date 1915 Aug	Hour	Summary of Events and Information	Remarks and references to Appendices
COISY	1		Billeted at COISY	
HEILLY	2	10 am	Marched to HEILLY	
"	3	5.30 pm	Rt X marched to MEAULTE	
MEAULTE	4		Requisitioned German trenches, we are now attached to 28th Bde RFA.	
		6.30 pm	Rt X came into action	
"	5		Dug new gun pit for C sub, built new O.B.	R.R.
"	6		do. do.	
"	7 to 22		Registered & do.	
"	23		do	
"	24	12 noon	Two H.E. shells dropped 10 x in rear of battery	
"	25		Quiet day.	
"	26	8.30 am	Changed Rt X with entrenchments of 123 battery.	
		7 pm	Fired at battery behind Pt 7770. who replied with 7 77mm shells.	
		12 mn	84th Bde took over from 28th Bde, who go into rest. A most happy time for a bit extra divisionl., no bickerings etc, everything going smoothly. OC 'Col' Sandys is happier in Bois Rond, and afraid them 3 weeks. Lt X came back to old place	
"	27	4 pm	Fired 4 rounds at enemy party in Bois Rond, & dispersed them.	
"	28	4 pm	Quiet day, until 7th German 77 mm shells were dropped on or within 50 yds of the battery; we replied on an of their batteries	

Army Form C. 2118

A/84

WAR DIARY
or
INTELLIGENCE SUMMARY
(Erase heading not required.)

Place	Date	Hour	Summary of Events and Information	Remarks and references to Appendices
MEAULTE	Aug 1915 30	4 pm	Germans shelled our Trenches with 10 small shell, we replied with 2 salvos on their trenches	
	31	10 am	Our Germans shelling our Trenches we fired on one of their batteries with rifles on us with a dozen 77 mm shells.	

Grant Cowper
OC A/84 R.F.A.

WAR DIARY
or
INTELLIGENCE SUMMARY

(Erase heading not required.)

Army Form C. 2118

Instructions regarding War Diaries and Intelligence Summaries are contained in F.S. Regs., Part II. and the Staff Manual respectively. Title Pages will be prepared in manuscript.

Place	Date	Hour	Summary of Events and Information	Remarks and references to Appendices
Coisy	30/7/15		Remained in camp. Instruction of specialists and exercising horses.	
Coisy	31/7/15		Remained in camp. Instruction of specialists and exercising horses.	
Coisy	1/8/15	10-30 a.m.	Church of England parade.	
Coisy	2/8/15	10-30 a.m. 4-30 p.m.	Battery marched out of COISY and arrived at HEILLY at 4-30 p.m.	
Heilly	3/8/15	9-15 a.m. 11-30 to 12-15	Capt Grant & Lt. Rice met O.C. 28th Brigade R.F.A. at MÉRICOURT l'ABBÉ. They then went to the wagon line, battery position and shewing station of the 12th French battery. Every line has explained by the Captain of the French battery who fired three rounds of melinite on a bridge registered points for the information of Capt. Grant and Lt Rice. They returned to HEILLY and brought up the right section and had left the position by 6 p.m. without being shelled. French still there, and some registered English officers to sleep, and wagon line. The position is between MÉAULTE and MÉRICOURT.	
		10 p.m.		
MÉAULTE	4/8/15	11 a.m.	Battery Right Section fired 18 registering rounds.	
		3 p.m.	Under slight artillery fire. "B" subsection gunpit was hit but no damage done. Left section came into form HEILLY and left its two guns on the position about 10 p.m. without being shelled.	
		10 p.m.		
MÉAULTE	5/8/15		No rounds fired by battery. Battery not under fire at all.	

J.J. Rice Capt.
RA 1st A/84 Bde.
RA 1st A/84 R.F.A.

18th Division

121/6607

"B"/84 Battery R.F.A.
Vol: I.
From 20 July to 31 Aug. 15

Army Form C. 2118

WAR DIARY
or
INTELLIGENCE SUMMARY
(Erase heading not required.)

Instructions regarding War Diaries and Intelligence Summaries are contained in F.S. Regs., Part II. and the Staff Manual respectively. Title Pages will be prepared in manuscript.

Place	Date 1915	Hour	Summary of Events and Information	Remarks and references to Appendices
Heytesbury	20 Jul		Battalion placed on war footing.	
"	26 "		Machine out & entrained at Warminster, right section 3/55 am left section 2/25 am. Embarked at Southampton in South West Milne & 2 Officers 44 other ranks in Mona Queen;	
Havre	27 "		Disembarked at Havre & left by our train at 6.19 pm.	
Longeau	28 "	5/30 AM	Detrained	
COISY	"	10 AM	Arrived by march route & now billeted in village.	

J.F. Morris Capt
Cmdg B/8th

Army Form C. 2118

WAR DIARY
or
INTELLIGENCE SUMMARY B/84 Bde RFA
(Erase heading not required.)

Instructions regarding War Diaries and Intelligence Summaries are contained in F.S. Regs., Part II. and the Staff Manual respectively. Title Pages will be prepared in manuscript.

Place	Date	Hour	Summary of Events and Information	Remarks and references to Appendices
CORSY	2/8/15	10AM	Battery marched with its train	
HEILLY	2/8/15	2PM	Battery arrived with its train & Firounaghue.	
"	3/8/15	7AM	Battery Comdr, 2 Offrs, 2 Orderlies went to BONNAY & thence to BRAY where the position of 1st Battery 28th Regt of French Artillery was reconnoitred with a view of taking over.	
"	"	8PM	Battery Staff & Left Section marched & arrived at gun position near BRONFAY FARM at 12 midnight.	
"	4/8/15	"	Right Section marched similarly	
BRAY	5/8/15	—	Situation is as follows:– 1 Gun in No 1 Casemate – French Batty. & 3 Guns in open concealed by branches, near BRONFAY FARM. Wagon line just S.W. of BRAY. F.O.O. in trenches ½ m NW of CARNOY. B.C. in Observing Station 500 yds SW of CARNOY. Battery registers on German trenches, its zone being from German trench 328 to Rly Halte at MAMETZ. 24 rounds fired.	
"	7/8/15	3AM	Battery took over cases after zero from 1/28th French Batty	Jus Morris Capt Cmdg B/84

1875. Wt. W593/826 1,000,000 4/15 J.B.C. & A. A.D.S.S. [Forms/C.2118.

WAR DIARY
or
INTELLIGENCE SUMMARY

Army Form C. 2118

B/84 Brigade R.F.A.

(Erase heading not required.)

Place	Date	Hour	Summary of Events and Information	Remarks and references to Appendices
BRONFAY FARM N. BRAY	8/8/15 to 14/8/15		Continued registration daily of enemy trenches, expending 73 rounds + 85 rounds during weeks ending 8th & 15th Aug. Enemy very quiet & apparently have not located Battery.	
	9/8/15	8.45 pm	Fired 3 rounds by request of FOO to check bomb throwers in front of our trench F2	
	10/8/15	9 pm	Fired 2 rounds for similar purpose. Started to dig new observing Station west of BOIS C.MFFET. & horse lines	
	11/8/15	—	Started to draw timber and improve gun emplacements. This is being done daily by all available manual labour	
	13/8/15	4 pm	German Sausage Balloon rose in neighbourhood of MONTAUBAN + was apparently engaged in observing the fire of an enemy battery whose target was about 3 m to south. It remained up till 7.15 pm. + registering was stopped by us.	

9 AM 14/8/15 to 15/8/15

J.A. Moran Capt.
O in dg B/84 Bde. R.F.A.

Army Form C. 2118

WAR DIARY
or
INTELLIGENCE SUMMARY
(Erase heading not required.)

B/84 Brigade RFA.

Place	Date	Hour	Summary of Events and Information	Remarks and references to Appendices
BRAY	14/8/15 to 21/8/15		Battery situated as during week before. Fired ammunition allotted, viz, 76 rounds Shrapnel 18pr, in registering zone of German trenches, and overlapping next battery from trench 345 on east to trench 311 on west, and in firing test rounds as required by Infantry, as follows:—	
	15/8/15		on trench F3. Time 3 min 17 secs	
	17"	5.15 pm	" " " 2 " 40 "	
	18"	3.45 PM	" F2 " " 13 " 0 "	— Telephone line interruption
	"	2.30 pm	" F1 " " 5 " 30 "	— Casemate in process of alteration
	"	11.30 pm	" F3 " " 3 " 15 "	
	19 "	4.5 pm	" 59 " " 2 " 3 "	
	20 "	4 Am	" 62 " " 1 " 15 "	
	"	5.41 pm	" 59 " " 1 " 58 "	
	21 "	3.40 Am	" " " " " 5 "	
			During week a new observing station was dug 300 yds west of BOIS CAFFET, the entrances of casemates were enlarged to increase traverse from 10 deg to between 30 and 40 deg, and a fire control dug out half completed in rear of casemates. Enemy quiet.	

J.H. Morris Capt
Cmdg B/84

WAR DIARY or INTELLIGENCE SUMMARY

Army Form C. 2118

Place	Date	Hour	Summary of Events and Information	Remarks and references to Appendices
Bronfay Farm	20/5	4 AM	Fired task over trench 62 at 4 am. 1 rnd 1 min 15 secs. Fired task on trench 59 at 5.41 pm. 1 rnd 1 min 58 secs. Expended 8 rounds in registration.	
		5.41pm	Continued digging fire control dug out.	
	21/5	3.40 AM	Fired 3.40 am over trench 59. 1 rnd 1 min 6 secs. Then 1 min 6 secs. Again at 4 hrs	
		4 pm	1 rnd 1 min 9 secs	
	22/5	11.30 AM	Wagon lines S.W. bank of BRAY was shelled by 9 shells, about 10.5 cm. From 11.30 am till 12.30 am. Seem of fire from PERONNE direction. No damage done and horses were shifted 400 yards S.W.	
	23/5	10.30 AM	Wagon lines had recently were shelled by about 20 shells. No damage. Began 10.30 am. Fired 16 rounds. Task over trench 59 at 4 pm.	
		4 pm	Same 1 min 4 secs	
	24/5	3.50pm	Task over 59 at 3.50 pm 1 min 1 min 30 sec	
		9.30pm	Noo 1 & 2 at Bronfay at 9.30 hrs and took over Noo 1 & 2 from 123 RFA at Bath	
		11 pm	11 pm near MEAULTE	
	25/5	10 AM	Handed over FOO an? Zone 355 to 3515 to all 15 Bd?s at 10 am. Handed over emplacements and dug out near Confay Farm and Zone 358 to 315 to 80 Bdy RFA at 8 pm. Marched at 8.30 pm to position near MEAULTE and took over emplacements and dug outs with Zone 435 to H.B. Right section had 35 rounds in magazine above Zone	
		8.30pm		

Army Form C. 2118

WAR DIARY
or
INTELLIGENCE SUMMARY
(Erase heading not required.)

Instructions regarding War Diaries and Intelligence Summaries are contained in F.S. Regs., Part II. and the Staff Manual respectively. Title Pages will be prepared in manuscript.

Place	Date	Hour	Summary of Events and Information	Remarks and references to Appendices
MEAULTE	26/8/15		Telephone line established to observe a factory just SW of MEAULTE	
			Osg. relieved with 21 rounds	
		5.30pm	Fired on hostile MG which is upset by MG officer to seem to which 25 shrapnel burst, who being	
		6.30pm	fired. No shrim with 3 rounds "air shrap" which silenced enemy gun.	
	28/8/15	6.30pm	Co. 24 slim with 16 rounds. Fired 2 salvoes (8 rounds) in line 483 to 485 at 6.30 hrs by order of O.C. B. 84 Bde RFA	

28/8/15

Jas Brown Capt
Cmdg B/84
RFA.

WAR DIARY
or
INTELLIGENCE SUMMARY
(Erase heading not required.)

Army Form C. 2118

B/84 RFA.

Place	Date	Hour	Summary of Events and Information	Remarks and references to Appendices
2300 yds ESE of MEAULTE	28/8/15	6.10pm	Enemy exploded camouflet & fired 12 77mm shell into trench 96. Battery fired 4 rounds in retaliation.	
	29/8/15		Enemy fired 12 77mm shell into trench 96 during day. Battery replied with 5 shrapnel.	
	30/8/15	5.15 AM	RE fired mine in front of trench 96. & Battery supported explosion with 8 rounds in 2 salvoes into trenches 483. 484. No German reply.	
		Various	German sausage balloon up all day over P.6. 45. 5.7 (estimated by range finder & compass) Battery fired 7 rounds in registration. & 16 rounds in retaliation for 12 rounds into our trench 96, and 7 rounds over into Battery, all 'minnies' & common 77 m.m. shell. Their effect Nil.	
	31/8/15	10.10 AM	Battery fired 8 rounds into trenches 282. 283. in reply to 7 German 77 m.m. shell into trench 98.	
	Daily 28 to 31 Aug		Digging a gun casemat for C/84. Cleaning and establishing wagon line in factory just S.W. of MEAULTE	

J. D. Moon Capt B/84.
12 noon 31-8-15.

121/6607

18th Division

"C"/84 Battery R.F.A.

Vol: I.

From 26 July to 31 Aug 15

Army Form C. 2118

WAR DIARY
or
INTELLIGENCE SUMMARY
(Erase heading not required.)

Place	Date	Hour	Summary of Events and Information	Remarks and references to Appendices
Nyl6berg	26/7/15	2.45	Intelligence Movements by section Bolton arrive Southampton by 9 A.M.	
Southampton	"	9 AM	Embarked on transport SS Mendian & left for Havre	
Havre	27/7/15	12 NN	Party in upper arrived at Havre & disembarked all personnel & private Mentian arrive by 4.30	
"	28/7/15	8 PM	Entrained Forts to Movements left for Rouen at 11.20 via Rouen & Amiens	
Longpre	29/7/15 today midnight		Again detrainment proceed at 1-40 pm by route to Corey	
Corey	29/7/15	4-30	Battalion in the village	

WAR DIARY
or
INTELLIGENCE SUMMARY
(Erase heading not required.)

Army Form C. 2118

Place	Date	Hour	Summary of Events and Information	Remarks and references to Appendices
COISY	Judy 30	4:30 pm	Went into billets. Warned during the night July 30/31st to prepare to move into action immediately	
COISY	31		Orders re. Action travelled during afternoon	
POISY	Aug 1		Church parade 10:30 am. Orders to move Monday morning to HEILLY received	
COISY	2		Brigade left COISY up to 10 a.m. No regret. arrived HEILLY 2:30 pm Bivouac just beyond outskirts of village. Orders received for half 103rd Battery to leave HEILLY at 7 pm Aug 3rd to take over positions occupied by French Batteries outside BRAY	
HEILLY	3		BCs of 103 & 128 Batteries & Staff left HEILLY 7 am for BONNAY. 2nd & 11th Batteries & OMAA proceeded from there with W. Staff to BRAY. Reconnoitred positions and discussed taking over same with French officers Col. Capt. Richards a hundred in this and met French officers & Officer of 3rd Battery was taking over new positions. (3rd Battery) having discussion re admirably appointing & guns into position in the open grounds in the open. Orders applied to Col Dufus Revelation 104. Left HEILLY 4 pm under Col. Donnan to take up position thereunder. Left the way after BRAY and eventually arrived at wagon lines at 2 am. Rd section brought from Rathey firing wagons into action in open spaces & received them with our	
BRAY	4		horses at 10 am. Left section left HEILLY at 9 pm & brought guns into action in our position 12 midnight. 2 Drivers from Coulmpers skipped over weglin lines.	
BRAY	5		Registered Coy 1st + guns after Run 10 a.m. – 3 pm. 29 Rounds fired	

Reached Leh. capture 17/8/14

WAR DIARY or INTELLIGENCE SUMMARY

Army Form C. 2118

Place	Date	Hour	Summary of Events and Information	Remarks and references to Appendices
E.N.E. BRAY	6.8.15	10.a.m to 1.30 p.m	O.C. C/84 visited Trench E 4 at request of O.C. Royal WEST KENTS found F.O.O. that night went to link up Trench and Observation Station by Telephone Battery	
do.	7.8.15		Proceeded further with registration. Expended 29 rounds. Relieved Trench battery not placed no firing in Front Gun Emplacements at 2.30 a.m. Telephone to F.O.O. satisfied 11.50 p.m. 2nd Lt STUART left position with Reserve information from O.C. Battle tho 2/Lt GIBBON went out on Sunday by 11.20 a.m. and reported Ammunition expended 24 rounds.	
do	8.8.15		2nd Lt GIBBON reported for duty from Am. Col. Complete registration of 7 units white shell fire (6 rounds) at 6.30 p.m. Several movements between Point 19 (334) registered at request of F.O.O. At no further regures first 2 rounds between 11.30 p.m. and 12.15 a.m. from shells and fire by enemy on position, but without casualty.	
do	9.8.15	6 a.m. to 10 p.m	There has been so concealy of any kind or importance of Ammunition	Monday
do	11.8.15	6 p.m	any improvement in the part of the enemy. Anthony of importance was received the Brigade major but Lieut Stone visited the Battery this afternoon. Two rounds were fired but as The salvos by the enemies were necessary & his men showing rotation as were registered and to continue.	Tuesday
do	12.8.15		Proceeded further with registration. Expended 28 rounds.	
do	13.8.15		Nothing to record General Cully weather Storm taking calls	

Army Form C. 2118

WAR DIARY
or
INTELLIGENCE SUMMARY
(Erase heading not required.)

Instructions regarding War Diaries and Intelligence Summaries are contained in F.S. Regs., Part II. and the Staff Manual respectively. Title Pages will be prepared in manuscript.

Place	Date	Hour	Summary of Events and Information	Remarks and references to Appendices
T.M. tramway	14.8.15	5.30	The enemy's batteries been given further registration turned ammunition in Maple trench & Sans Nom. Shrapnel sent light over Maple & burnt just over	Kemler
	15.8.15		Proceeding further with registration and expended 14 rounds.	(T.M.)
	16.8.15		No action on the part of the enemy, very quiet all along the line. Got some very wonderful shots at 11.35 p.m. Time 1.10	Out
	17.8.15	6.30	Another unsuccessful day since registering some on the line now. Nothing new. Weather cool.	Kemler Ruddell
	18.8.15	7.30 pm	No action on the part of the enemy. Batteries on left remained to fire. Weather fine but colder	Ruddell
	19.8.15	7 p.m	Nothing to report except counter-battery registering	Kemler Ruddell
	20.8.15	7 -	Nothing to report. - very quiet on both fronts. Weather fine	
	21.8.15		Nothing to report. Battery took on Trench "J". Train 23 rounds.	(T.M.)
	22.8.15	6.30	Very quiet. Received a visit from the Officers of the Battery who are relieving us & instructions as to mover. N. Oldham has gone on to see the new position.	Kemler Ruddell
	23.8.15	9 a.m	Nothing to report. Battery did not register. Weather good.	J.H.

WAR DIARY
or
INTELLIGENCE SUMMARY
(Erase heading not required.)

Army Form C. 2118

Place	Date	Hour	Summary of Events and Information	Remarks and references to Appendices
E.N.E. BRAY	24/8	6.20.	Nothing fresh on the front. The O.C. visited the new position & recommended that the wagon lines. It was found that the gun emplacements were not available for the guns allotted. Reported to our G.H.Q. No ammunition expended	Weather
AILLIETTE	25/8	10.h. a.m.	Very quiet. We visited by General Chetwynd, who in turn inspected him emplacement + limbs. The sections of both the left section were reviewed on 24/8 1 — at 9pm to 50th Bde. The 12th at MEAULTE. The Right Section returned to night at 6.30 and both in position at sunrise from A/54. Weather improved.	airway Powder
MEAULTE	26/8	8.45	Battery did not fire. At 6h.a.m. the position was shelled. Ten shells dropped just within range of the Battery. No casualties. The shells were cover were light & shrapnel. Weather fine.	
—	27/8	10 pm	No ammunition expended. Received an instruction to change our emplacement not A/54 and to build new emplacements for guns to fire from new positions to cover the guns required on from 30 to 49 E.	
—	28/8	16 pm	Have registered to front on gun allotted to A/54 new refitted areas to H.S. Have moved a firm in ordinary use 8/14 as ordered. Have carried plans of new Battery from lorries + communication trenches from ordinary — to see Ammunition Exp. 11 rounds.	Sundries

1875 Wt. W593/826 1,000,000 4/15 J.B.C. & A. A.D.S.S./Forms/C. 2118.

Army Form C. 2118

WAR DIARY
or
INTELLIGENCE SUMMARY
(Erase heading not required.)

Instructions regarding War Diaries and Intelligence Summaries are contained in F.S. Regs., Part II. and the Staff Manual respectively. Title Pages will be prepared in manuscript.

Place	Date	Hour	Summary of Events and Information	Remarks and references to Appendices
Menil	29/8	noon	All 7" Batteries are busy in building gun emplacements for new position. No action taken today on our own initiative. The enemy shelled the position principally, also 2 to the right of them and in front from 4 pm to 6 pm intermittently, about 30 rounds in all.	
	30/8	5-30	Nothing of moment occurred and took in action on gun emplacements and completed. Enemy shelled as usual 97 m/m at 10.30 - 2.24 - 2-30	
	31/8	6 pm	Nothing of moment occurred and took no action as gun emplacements not complete. Enemy shelled as usual 97 m/m at 10.15 am.	

121/6607

18th Division

"D"/84 Battery R.F.A.

Vol: I

From 20. Feb & Aug. 15

A2
Also

Army Form C. 2118

WAR DIARY
or
INTELLIGENCE SUMMARY
(Erase heading not required.)

Instructions regarding War Diaries and Intelligence Summaries are contained in F.S. Regs., Part II. and the Staff Manual respectively. Title Pages will be prepared in manuscript.

Place	Date	Hour	Summary of Events and Information	Remarks and references to Appendices
Hey Canbury	20/2/15		The battery was placed on a war footing.	
"	26/2/15		The battery LyC & proceeded overseas as follows:	
		6 a.m.	Rifle section	
		7.30 a.m.	Kit section	
			The battery entrainer at Hounslow and proceeded to Southampton to join on the Battalion. The battery embarked as follows:	
			2 of C.C. Carver in the "Gloria Queen."	
			34 men under Lt. C.C. Carver in the "Gloria Queen."	
			Remainder of the battery under Capt. C.F. Andrew in S.S. Southwark.	
Havre	27/2/15	10 a.m.	The battery began to disembark and on completion of disembarkation at 3 pm moved off by road to S. Camp where the night was spent.	
"	28/2/15	12 noon	The battery entrained at Pt 4 Gare handaveu	
		3.0 p.m.	Train left Havre.	
"	29/2/15	11 a.m.	The battery detrained at Longueau and marched by road to Croÿ arriving there about 10 a.m. Officers were billeted in the village.	
Croÿ	30/2/15	10 a.m.	The battery moved from Croÿ into bivouac at Pernoy.	

E. Andrew
Capt. R.F.A.
O.C. D/84

WAR DIARY
or
INTELLIGENCE SUMMARY
(Erase heading not required.)

Army Form C. 2118

D/84th Bde.

Place	Date	Hour	Summary of Events and Information	Remarks and references to Appendices
COISY	Aug 2.1915 2.8.15	10 a.m.	The battery moved from bivouac at COISY by road to HEILLY and then went into bivouac.	
HEILLY	5.8.15	10 a.m.	The battery moved by road from HEILLY to BURE-SUR-ANCRE and became the 27th Brigade R.F.A. forming the right group of the 9th Divisional Artillery	
BURE	6.8.15	7.45 p.m.	The right section proceeded by road to SUZANNE and took up a position on the south east side of the SUZANNE - MARICOURT road, where the wagon line of the SUZANNE. The wagon line was established on the south east side of the CAPPY - SUZANNE road some 800 yards from SUZANNE.	
SUZANNE	7.8.15	12.30 pm	Registration of German trenches began.	
"	8.8.15	11.00 a.m.	Registration on German trenches continued.	

E. S. Sutton
Captain

D/84th Bde RFA

WAR DIARY or INTELLIGENCE SUMMARY
Army Form C. 2118

Place	Date	Hour	Summary of Events and Information	Remarks and references to Appendices
SUZANNE	9/8/15	10 a.m.	The left section arrived at the battery position from BRAY and the 6th French Battery took over departure.	
"	10/8/15	3 p.m.	22 rounds shrapnel were fired to obtain parallel lines.	
		5.30 p.m.	H. round shrapnel were fired to gets lines I₂	
"	11/8/15	3.30 p.m.	18 rounds " " " Point 473 and 19	
"	12/8/15	6.45 p.m.	A German aeroplane was observed from the battery.	
		5pm to 6 pm	Four kites were observed to hover high over Pt 37. Hostile battery in the left front.	
"	13/8/15	10 p.m. midnight	H. shell was fired at the village of HARDECOURT on enemy front line. 8 rounds. were fired at point 1100 on suspect of machine gun firing HR MARICOURT	
"	14/8/15	1.40 p.m.	A working party was observed at R13 3/7 and shelled by 10 rounds shrapnel.	
		2.40 p.m.	Vehicle was observed on the road running S.E. in R14 and shelled by 119th Battery. English aeroplanes were very active during the day. A German aeroplane was observed.	
"	15/8/15	8.30 p.m.	300 rounds were fired on trench works in square 164 at square quadrant.	
		11.30 a.m.	Many rounds were fired at Point in trench work west of Point 100 yards from W. end of wood on approach.	
		11 a.m.	Enfilade rounds	
		11.35 a.m.	to system S. end of wood H.3. Point 246 at Q.10 Curve round " " of Point 157 on R.18	
		5 p.m.	The enemy fired H. shells at our fire line trenches on Péronne Road. He was observed that the enemy are constructing a supper trench from trenches of Pt 1.	
"	15/8/15	11.24 a.m.	6 rounds we fired at an enemy lamb purser party at Point 464.	
"	18/8/15	9 a.m.	6 rounds were fired at point 457 to front correction and to check lines. No enemy aeroplanes were observed nor was his artillery active.	

Army Form C. 2118

WAR DIARY
or
INTELLIGENCE SUMMARY
(Erase heading not required.)

Instructions regarding War Diaries and Intelligence Summaries are contained in F.S. Regs., Part II. and the Staff Manual respectively. Title Pages will be prepared in manuscript.

Place	Date	Hour	Summary of Events and Information	Remarks and references to Appendices
SUZANNE	16/8/15	6.15 a.m.	2 rounds shrapnel were fired as fuse 464 to check registration	
	17/8/15	10 a.m.	Captive balloon was seen at Flaucourt. (Bearing 180° Mag. 229° Mag. 235° Mag. the front at Suzanne is two Colza factory Rivet.	
		3.15 p.m.	2 rounds shrapnel fired in east at point I, (N. of 442)	
	18/8/15	11.40 a.m.	Working parties seen observing the day in Q.22 and R.19.	
		11.50 a.m.	8 rounds shrapnel fired at wood between ? not used. 40 at intervals of 2 hrs, bring in Curlu wood	
		12.30 p.m.		en communication trench at G3
			at fire trench in front of I,	to igniter shrapnel not against enemy
		3.30 p.m.	2 salvos of H rounds were fired at the Bois des Menil.	
		11.30 p.m.	3 rounds shrapnel	at point I. to register
		12.38 a.m.	2 rounds	at ?
	19/8/15			fired 402 for a tree
		3.26 p.m.	During the afternoon the enemy shelled our ? support trenches at the S. end of Peronne Road	
			4 rounds shrapnel were fired as a test at fuse 457.	
		3.30 p.m.	3 rounds	to ignite CAVALIER in Q.23
		3.40 p.m.	3 rounds	fuse 442
		4 p.m.		at fuse 457 as test
		4 p.m.	4 rounds	to disperse working party S. of cross roads in R.13
		6.30 p.m.	1 salvo of 4 guns	at Q.5.6/4 for observation by aeroplane
		7 p.m.		at barrier on Peronne road
	20/8/15	11 a.m.	3 salvos of 4 guns	at fuse 457 as test
			1 round shrapnel	
	21/8/15	11.30 a.m.	Working parties were again observed in Q.22 and near Curlu wood	
		4.15 p.m.	20 rounds shrapnel were fired on German trenches between points 2634 and 275, at fuses 462 as a test	

1875 Wt. W 593/826 1,000,000 4/15 J.B.C. & A. A.D.S.S./Forms/C. 2118.

Army Form C. 2118

D/84: Bde. R.F.A.

WAR DIARY
or
INTELLIGENCE SUMMARY
(Erase heading not required.)

Instructions regarding War Diaries and Intelligence Summaries are contained in F. S. Regs., Part II. and the Staff Manual respectively. Title Pages will be prepared in manuscript.

Place	Date	Hour	Summary of Events and Information	Remarks and references to Appendices
SUZANNE	21/8/15	3 p.m.	A working party was observed in Q 13. 3.7.	
"	22/8/15	8 a.m.	16 rounds shrapnel were fired by observation by aeroplane.	
		6.15 p.m.	A German captive balloon was observed W. of MARICOURT	
"	23/8/15		During the morning and early afternoon the enemy shelled our support trenches and the 118? Battery on our right.	
"	"	3.30 p.m.	10 rounds shrapnel were fired at trench on Bronze Road by sect. of 21 Siege pn.	
"	24.8.15	12.10 a.m.	S.O.S. at working party in Y wood.	
		9.45 p.m.	Heavy H.E. registration was performed by a section of R. Siege R.M.A. and in addition 15 rounds of armour piercing as P 14 30/85, striking the picture of a section of our B.G.	
"	25.8.15	3 p.m.	One eye section fired 10 rounds shrapnel at a mounting gun in Q 10. 45/55	
			The right section fired 31 rounds " " to report various points in the new work, observed to 22.	
MEAULTE			being V7 point 485 R 198. The ammunition was supplied by the Siege Battery.	
SUZANNE	26/8/15	8.45 p.m.	The left section was relieved and enabled to open the right section on the registration	
MEAULTE	27/8/15 12 noon		15 rounds shrapnel were fired to reports further points to observe numerous guns	
"	"	6 p.m.	9 rounds " " " opened and beheld the enemy's [illegible] trenches by Italian	
			hosty firing on FRICOURT and CONTALMAISON	
"	28/8/15	2 a.m.	The enemy shells numbers 86 + 87 and as relatives buffing to voluere wounds found two 486, 487,	
		6.45 p.m.	A German shrapnel flying low, approached him over MAMETZ, crossed to the right over MEAULTE and returned by the line of approach. It was engaged by our anti-aircraft gun without success.	
"	29/8/15	4 p.m.	14 rounds shrapnel were fired to register point A: [illegible] line limit W of aeroplane hubs and B: [illegible] feature 9171 and 6959.	
			While registering was proceeding the battery on our right was [illegible] Our rounds fire from 10 yards to the west of our No 1 gun but the majority fell somewhere between these [illegible]	

1875 Wt. W593/826 1,000,000 4/15 J.B.C. & A. A.D.S.S./Forms/C. 2118.

Army Form C. 2118

D184 - Bde R.F.A.
(4)

WAR DIARY
or
INTELLIGENCE SUMMARY
(Erase heading not required.)

Instructions regarding War Diaries and Intelligence Summaries are contained in F.S. Regs., Part II. and the Staff Manual respectively. Title Pages will be prepared in manuscript.

Place	Date	Hour	Summary of Events and Information	Remarks and references to Appendices
MEAULTE	30.8.18	6 a.m.	A German captive balloon observed over CONTAMAISON remained up in air all day.	
		8.30 a	Three German aeroplanes flew over our lines from East to West. Two below were engaged by our anti-aircraft guns.	
		10 am		
		9.15 am	The balloon in our sight was shelled, four rounds white bursting near them. However did not explode.	
			3 rounds shrapnel were fired on horses in Ravine in line maps one 487.	
		3.10 pm	1 round shrapnel was fired at German lines. P 3 6/8.	
		3.35 pm	The enemy fired 2 rounds above fire which were the most unpleasant being short of E Battery.	
		5.15 pm	Enemy's shrapnel were fired as reprisal of firing 9171 and we fired bursts 1/1.	
		6.30 pm	6 rounds shrapnel were fired towards German supports trenches	
		6.45 pm	The enemy artillery fires 14 rounds air 13 battery probably shrapnel from 977 Battery. Whilst the shelling was going on two air-planes were observed to circle over MEAULTE and circle off in the direction of BECOURT.	
		6.45 p.m.	Flash located about 9171 L 30 of Battalion which shells 96 the daily Flash located 8° of 9163 Contramaison Flash, 9 Machine Gun located about pt 477	
	31.8.18	8.40 am	Enemy 21 rds J 7.7 fired into our trenches from trenches J 9171. 31 rds of 7.7 fired shorty of the position from Bronze Battery.	
		10 am	15 rds Shrapnel fire into German post 2nd line trench between 483-496 in retaliation.	
		10.30 am	(1 9 10 7.) on our support trench and "BENTE" Redoubt. Smoke balloon up all 30° + 31°? blue CONTRAMAISON. The balloon are see whilst of 84 Alba prisoner.	

E. Sometime
Lt.Col...Capt?

12/7051

18th Division

84th Brigade R.F.A.
Vol: 3

Sept. 15

WAR DIARY
or
INTELLIGENCE SUMMARY 84 Brigade R.F.A.

September 1915

Army Form C. 2118.

Place	Date	Hour	Summary of Events and Information	Remarks and references to Appendices
MEAULTE	15th to 17th	6 p.m.	The four Batteries, A, B, C, D, in casemates 1½ miles S.E. of MEAULTE with C/85 (How'rs) formed left Group of 18 Divnl Artillery and covered sectors of our trenches R2b and R2d. — An average of 12 rounds per Battery were fired daily for retaliation and registration; rounds recd from Germans was (mostly) of 8-15. German 77 m.m. "5.9" shells; no casualties - daily, with occasional 5.9 shell. On reorganization of our Defence, A, B and D Batteries with C/85 formed the Centre Group, 18 Divnl Arty : H.Q. in MEAULTE. A/84. 8/84, and C/85 remained in same casemates. 10/84.	
	17th			

WAR DIARY or INTELLIGENCE SUMMARY

Army Form C. 2118

84 Brigade R.F.A. Cont'd

68

Place	Date	Hour	Summary of Events and Information	Remarks and references to Appendices
MEAULTE 23 and 24 ALBERT 25			Took over casemates 400x E. of BELLEVUE FARM, AL- BERT - Work on Alternative Positions was com- menced. A/84. supporting Battery for R3 Sector; B/84. supporting Battery for E Sector; A/84 Re- inforcing B/Sgt. Battery for the North Sectors - C/84 was in support. 367 Coy R.F.A. attached. In view of probable advance from our R3 and E3 Sectors Batteries were heavily engaged in bombardment of Sap heads, M.G. Emplace- ments & in wire cutting -	
	26 / / 30		Ammunition only allowed for retaliation purposes	

WAR DIARY
or
INTELLIGENCE SUMMARY 84 Bde R.F.A. — Cont

Army Form C. 2118

Place	Date	Hour	Summary of Events and Information	Remarks and references to Appendices
TREUX	30		Bde. A.W. continued at same place for war this month.	6.3

R. English. Col:
C.O. 84 Bde. R.F.A.

Copy.

G.S.

XVIII Division.

Mining Report, TAMBOUR DU CLOS.

1. Progress fair.

2. Enemy heard approaching very close to G.4 near junction of G.4 and the transversal.

Camouflet fired 10:3 p.m. on 16.9.15. Charge 1000 lbs. guncotton. No crater was visible. Our artillery fired 2 shells.

17/9/15.

sd. G.W. Wellesley, Captain R.E.
O.C. 178th Tunnelling Co. R.E.

2.

18th/Div/G

Head Quarters,

55th. Infantry Brigade.

For information.
In future O.C.178th.Tunnelling Co. will send reports direct to you.

17th. September 1915.

Lieut-Colonel.
Sen.Gen.Staff Officer,18th. Div.

121/7593

18th Hussars

84th Bde: R.F.A.
vol 4

Oct 15

Army Form C. 2118

WAR DIARY
or
INTELLIGENCE SUMMARY
(Erase heading not required.)

84th Bde. A.E.A.

Place	Date	Hour	Summary of Events and Information	Remarks and references to Appendices
NEAULT	October 1915		During the month the Brigade remained in action in the same position as occupied and under the same organization as arranged on Sept. 17th 1915. — The enemy has been fairly quiet on the whole — Trench mortars being his most oppressive weapon; but these have been well kept under by our own artillery fire — Our allotment of ammunition has been small but sufficient to retaliate effectively as occasion required — Positions in rear have been prepared and the present position much improved during the month; much labour, material and ingenuity having been expended — The waggon lines also have been got ready for the approaching winter — Leave to England was granted for 8 days commencing Oct. 28th and is to continue; only a very small number of men being allowed to go at one time —	

Army Form C. 2118

WAR DIARY
or
INTELLIGENCE SUMMARY
(Erase heading not required.)

Instructions regarding War Diaries and Intelligence Summaries are contained in F.S. Regs., Part II. and the Staff Manual respectively. Title Pages will be prepared in manuscript.

Place	Date	Hour	Summary of Events and Information	Remarks and references to Appendices
	Oct 20th		Col. C.E. English proceeded to England. He had commanded the Brigade since it was raised at Colchester in Oct 1914, including 3 months active service in France. Major (temp. Lt.Col.) D.J. Ashris R.F.A. from 65th Howitzer Battery ~V Div succeeded him in command of the Brigade —	
	Oct 21st		Lt.Col. F.W. LEMER c/84 proceeded home — Capt. M.A. Stocking R.F.A. from 46th Div joined to command c/84 —	

B.J. Ashris Lt. Col.
Cmdg. 84th Bde R.F.A.

31.10.15

18th Division

84th Bde. R.F.A.
Vol. 5

121/7693

Nov. 15

Army Form C. 2118

84th Brigade I.S. D-4

WAR DIARY
or
INTELLIGENCE SUMMARY
(Erase heading not required.)

Place	Date	Hour	Summary of Events and Information	Remarks and references to Appendices
MEAULTE	1/12/15 NOVEMBER 1915.		During the month, Both armies in action same positions + covered same zone. Enemy fairly quiet on the whole, trench mortars & lo hitzdrangs continue to annoy however, but there have been well their under, by our artillery. Been allotment of ammunition has been slightly increased. Heavy rains during the month have caused considerable labour in keeping trenches & dug outs in repair; dug outs and some for stables have been completely overroads accomodation in wagon lines & R.A.C. considerably improved. Leave to England continues. The number granted have been increased. The French Military decoration (Croix de Guerre) has been awarded to No 15 36. Gunner W.G. Coton I/84. Sergt I.F.C. 3rd Army for gallant conduct. No casualties. 1-12-15.	Rowble Lt Col OC Comdg 84 Bde I.S. Ja

84th Bde. 87a.
vol: 6

121/7809

18th Division

Rec 15

WAR DIARY
or
INTELLIGENCE SUMMARY
(Erase heading not required.)

Army Form C. 2118

Place	Date	Hour	Summary of Events and Information	Remarks and references to Appendices
MÉAULTE	Dec: 1915		During the month, Bde renewed in action in the same position as last month and covered the same zones which are, as before, held by 55th Inf Brigade.— The first week was very wet and much work had to be done to keep the dug-outs et finally habitable — the enemy was similarly engaged the front being quiet as regards shelling. —	
	Dec: 18th		Two Batteries of 4th Welsh Hoo RFA (T) 53rd Div having recently arrived from England occupied two of our alternate positions under instruction of our Batteries. They remained about 5 days and fired a few rounds.	
	Dec: 25th		Divine Service was held in a barn at DERNANCOURT and was attended by about 200 men of the Bde — Batteries arranged with help of gifts from home to celebrate Xmas as well as circumstances would allow — No truce of any sort was granted to the enemy — In conjunction with R.E. and 8th East Surrey Regt. works were obtained by the continued artillery fire of the Bde after exploding a mine near FRICOURT	
	Dec: 16th		A heavy artillery bombardment which included 9".2 took place on FRICOURT Tambour Bde assisted —	

WAR DIARY
or
INTELLIGENCE SUMMARY
(Erase heading not required.)

Army Form C. 2118

Place	Date	Hour	Summary of Events and Information	Remarks and references to Appendices
MEAULTE	Dec. 29th		Enemy shelled our Trenches heavily in the evening — He attempted a small enterprise on our right — under cover of three shells —	
	Dec. 30th		A similar mining exploit continued with artillery as on 28th — Casualties in D/84 one N.C.O. died 3 wounded, two men wounded accidentally	
			During the month Lieut T.H. Davison C/84 was promoted to Capt and sent to 8th Div. Waggon lines have been still further improved as regards shelters and standings, but the wet weather has increased the mud everywhere —	

MEAULTE
1.1.16.

Lyndon Lt Col RFA
Cmdg 84th Bde RFA

84th Bde: R.F.A.
Vol: 7
Jan '16

1st Div

Army Form C. 2118

WAR DIARY
or
INTELLIGENCE SUMMARY
(Erase heading not required.)

Instructions regarding War Diaries and Intelligence Summaries are contained in F.S. Regs., Part II. and the Staff Manual respectively. Title Pages will be prepared in manuscript.

Place	Date	Hour	Summary of Events and Information	Remarks and references to Appendices
MEAULTE	January 3rd 1916		During the month, Bde remains in action in same position as last month, 9 covered zones, which are as before held by 65th Inf. Bde.	
	6"		168th Bde. Tracey R.F.A. 32nd Div Art. occupied alternate position & remained in action 14 days under instruction of the Battery of whose alternate position was occupied.	
	8"	6pm	A Group shoot in conjunction with 60 pdr & 6" Siege was carried out on front trench line trenches North of FRICOURT. under the direction of B.G. R.A. 18 Div.	
	12		C/164 R.F.A. 32nd Div Art. (Howitzer) was attached to Howitzer Battery & Group & occupied that Battery's alternate position for 14 days. A Group shoot was carried out in morning commencing at 11 am on Enemy's emplacements N.W. FRICOURT. Enemy retaliation on our front line trenches. This shoot returns very effective. The German dug in which emplacements were situated.	
	14		English Aeroplane fell just behind our front trenches N.W. FRICOURT. Enemy fired 77 m.m. shell at it. burnt. B/84 fired shrapnel at enemy front line at men looking over parapet. Observer pilot got away wounded.	

1875 Wt. W593/826 1,000,000 4/15 J.B.C. & A. A.D.S.S./Forms/C. 2118.

WAR DIARY or INTELLIGENCE SUMMARY

Army Form C. 2118

Place	Date	Hour	Summary of Events and Information	Remarks and references to Appendices
MEAULTE	22		Group shoot on enemy trench. Second line trench. Most apparent satisfactory	
	27	7pm	Gas alarm was given but no trace was noticed in Battn in our zone. It was afterwards ascertained the alarm emanated from 48th Div on our left, who had been fired on by Lachrymatory shells.	
	29	6am	Gas alarm. Faint smell for some distance behind line. Lachrymatory and sight on whole of our zone.	

During month, considerable improvement has been made in wagon lines, horse standings, billets. Also Bty. O.C. (officer at TREUX). Altinere positions improved mostly by having horses attacked during them. The month has been much more active as regards artillery on both sides. Adjustment of ammunition increased.

Lt. Col. D. G. Blois R.F.A. Comdg 84th Bde. awarded. D.S.O.

J.J. Phin — Lt Col R.F.A
Comdg 84 Bde R.F.A

2.7.16

84th Bde: R.F.A.
Vol: 8

WAR DIARY or INTELLIGENCE SUMMARY

84TH BRIGADE ROYAL FIELD ARTILLERY

Reg. No. 1/3/16

Place	Date	Hour	Summary of Events and Information	Remarks and references to Appendices
MÉAULTE	1916 Jan 31st		A heavy bombardment took place at about 5.15pm on the front held covered by B/84 and to our left - B/84 kept up a very efficient barrage and prevented enemy from entering our trenches, for which the thanks of O.C. 55th Inf Bde were received. Enemy was never successful in the trenches to our left and took a few prisoners.	
	Feb 3rd		We exploded a mine and experimented with artillery fire.	
	Feb 6th		7th Div came up and took over the right half of our front which involved the following moves — A/84 after being in action in the same position for six months withdrew to BUIRE — C/84 withdrew to BUIRE — D/84 shoot foot lost is to B/84 shoot foot — C/84 withdrew to BUIRE — D/84 in the support of E, which is the only part of the front that reinforce B/84 in the support of E — C/85 withdraws and is replaced by D/85 in a new cover — slightly different position also to cover E — This group therefore now becomes "R" group and consists of B/84 D/84 and D/85, with A/84 & C/84 in reserve at BUIRE — B.A.C. from TROUX to BUIRE — Waggon lines from VILLE to BUIRE — The 7th Div Artillery then took over	

WAR DIARY
or
INTELLIGENCE SUMMARY

Army Form C. 2118

(Erase heading not required.)

Place	Date	Hour	Summary of Events and Information	Remarks and references to Appendices
MEAULTE	1916 Feb 11th		The right portion of our line was 14th Div R.H.A (F and T. Batteries) and 31st Howitzer Battery R.F.A – We are now therefore in the extreme right of the X Corps and support E, infantry so held by 55th Inf Bde – E, sector is about one mile N.W. of FRICOURT – Enemy shelled the extreme left of 7th Div very heavily from 5 till 7 pm. Germans attempted a raid with about 100 men to the trenches and during same shafts – no attempts was entirely unsuccessful and they lost approximately 200 casualties. D/84 and D/85 cooperated with a quick rate of fire in accordance with a scheme previously prepared and no afterwards received the thanks of 7th Div for our assistance. Both batteries were heavily shelled but fire was kept up without difficulty –	
	Feb 12th 1916		A similar but less intense bombardment took place about ½ mile further south – D/84 and D/85 again assisted in repelling this second attack which was less determined than that of 2nd and was dispersed by machine gun fire –	

Army Form C. 2118

WAR DIARY
or
INTELLIGENCE SUMMARY
(Erase heading not required.)

Instructions regarding War Diaries and Intelligence Summaries are contained in F.S. Regs., Part II. and the Staff Manual respectively. Title Pages will be prepared in manuscript.

Place	Date	Hour	Summary of Events and Information	Remarks and references to Appendices
MEAULTE	1916 Feb 1-29		During the month enemy was slightly more active but was kept well in hand by snipers and artillery support. Weather fine until 3 days of heavy rain about Feb. 26th - Leave was continued to England until stopped on Feb 24th - Horses suffered by moving in Feb 6th to unsheltered wagon lines from the huts that had been so carefully constructed in BRAY VILLE sur ANCRE - Casualties :- One man killed and two wounded in D/84 Bde. T.F.A. Officers joining Bde :- Capt H.W.S. Wright R.A.M.C., 2/Lt. S.E. Tennant R.F.A., T.F. 2/Lt J.E.A. Platts R.F.A.(S.R.) and 2/Lt R.G. Saunders R.F.A.(S.R.) Officers departure :- Capt. G.D. Yates R.A.M.C. to 55th Field Ambulance.	

MEAULTE March 1st 1916.

[signature] Lt Col RFA

Cmdg. 84 & 128 RFA Z

84 RFA
vol 9

Volume 9.

WAR DIARY
or
INTELLIGENCE SUMMARY
(Erase heading not required.)

Army Form C. 2118

84TH BDE, R.F.A.
March 1916

Place	Date	Hour	Summary of Events and Information	Remarks and references to Appendices
MEAULTE	1/63		B/84 & J/84 in action in support & reinforcing E/1 Subsector. The Bdes was relieved by 165th Bde R.F.A.	
	4		Marched to rest billets at DAOURS.	
DAOURS	9.		C/84 went into action close to SUZANNE, & attached to 30th Div arty. Remainder of Bde remaining at DAOURS, until 20th March. During this time the weather was favourable for drill purposes, Batteries refitted & daily drills was carried out under Battery & Bde arrangements. Freedom of movement was welcome by all ranks after the long sojourn "in the line"	
	20.		March Command for SUZANNE, where Bde went into action as that of Right Group R.A. 30th Div. Commanded by O.C. 149 Bde R.F.A. Relief was complete & Major Right Group R.A. 153 div was taken over by O.C. 54 Bde at 10 a.m. 22 March. This group consists of A/4 Battery 54 Bde R.F.A. D/151 Bde D/149. Battery T.F.A. (15 pr). A/83. 9 C/85 Batteries T.F.A. (4.5 How). L.e. T.F.A. (4.5 How) in support of 56th Inf Bde Holding Y Sector from SOMME CANAL (South) to northern edge of X WOOD (north). H.Q. of group was situated in CHATEAU SUZANNE. From occupying new position until end of month. German artillery was fairly active. Our ammunition was very much restricted, but strict instruction was issued to reply by end of month. Casualties 3 men D/84 wounded by German shell fire.	

Army Form C. 2118

WAR DIARY
or
INTELLIGENCE SUMMARY
(Erase heading not required.)

March 1916

Instructions regarding War Diaries and Intelligence Summaries are contained in F.S. Regs., Part II. and the Staff Manual respectively. Title Pages will be prepared in manuscript.

Place	Date	Hour	Summary of Events and Information	Remarks and references to Appendices
SUZANNE	31		Officers joining Bde. 2/L R.S. Bowman to II/34 from DAC. 19-3-16. " " " 2/L S.E. Tarrant T.F.to 4/4 Surrey Co. T.F. 24-3-16. Promotion: Capt. G.w.S. Norris Comdg B/54. to Major. (16 Hos.) Gazette 30-3-16. The Brigade is still in 18th Division &c. and forms part of XIII Army Corps with 7 & 30th Divisions - This Corps - part of 4 Army - holds front of "Right group" which is the most Southerly group of the Expeditionary Force; a French Colonial Division joining on our immediate right with the other SOMME between us.	
	3-4-16			

Signed,
Lieut Col RFA
Commanding 84th Bde RFA

Army Form C. 2118

XVIII VOL 10
84 R.F.A.

WAR DIARY
or
INTELLIGENCE SUMMARY
(Erase heading not required.)

84th Bde R.F.A.   April 1916.

Place	Date	Hour	Summary of Events and Information	Remarks and references to Appendices
SUZANNE	April 1916.		The Brigade forming part of Right Group Art 18 Division commanded by O.C. 84th Bde. Remained in action during the month supporting same front. Enemy artillery fairly active. Gun registration which let the former 54th Bde. front on our right & centre Groups Art 18 New on our left sometimes operated apparent to dominate Enemy arty fire in some locality but a different front have been prepared for possible evacuation on own future occasion. D/149 Bde R.F.A. was relieved by C/149 on night 14/15. Casualties during month. Killed. O.R. 1 Wounded. Lieut. G.L. Carré. T/84. R.F.A. O.R. 8. PROMOTIONS. 2nd Lt. Taylor C/84	2nd Lieut. Leslie Simon 3/84s	b. Temp Lieut. 5-4-16. Departures 2/Lieut WG Aceson A/84 to V/15 Trench Mortar Battery 25-4-16. " " Rees. Saunderson B OC. to 2/15 Trench Mortar Battery 14-4-16.	

WAR DIARY
INTELLIGENCE SUMMARY

84th Bde R.F.A.   April 1916.

Place: SUZANNE

About 27th April the 55th Hy. Bde were relieved by 90th Hy Bde 30th Div (County Palatine) and we continued to to support the same front —

Byslin [T] W. RFA
Cundy 84 to Bde RFA.

May 1st 1916

VOLUME 12

Army Form C. 2118

WAR DIARY
or
INTELLIGENCE SUMMARY
(Erase heading not required.)

XVIII

84th Bde R.F.A. VOL II

Place	Date	Hour	Summary of Events and Information	Remarks and references to Appendices
SUZANNE	May 1916		Situated as last month.	
			Enemy artillery still very active, on night of 5th French lines on our immediate right. South of Somme very heavily shelled at 2.50 A.M. 6th. Enemy commenced shelling Suzanne - Maricourt Valley 11/84 although having no casualties had a close vicinity Battery. O.C. this Battery especially mentions an act of gallantry & devotion to duty of No 5449 Gunner Stort who when his telephone failed at act at once brought another telephone like ground, the road to cross being heavily shelled at the time, he succeeded in re-establishing communication.	
		5th 6th 7th		
		12th	Bde was relieved by 149 (County Palatine) Bde R.F.A. & marched into first billets at ARGOEUVES. One Battery B/84 & B.a.c. to St Sauveur.	
			Leaving 9 strike were commenced on 12th to continue progressing for remainder of month.	
		17th	On re-organisation of Divl Art. (aut G.H.Q. O.B./315 dat 6-5-16) Bde was transferred complete to 18th D.A.C. to be known in future as No 3 Division D.A.C. Capt. R.P. Constable commanding.	
			Officers: 2nd Lieut. J.E. Pearlie.	

WAR DIARY
or
INTELLIGENCE SUMMARY

(Erase heading not required.)

Army Form C. 2118

Place	Date	Hour	Summary of Events and Information	Remarks and references to Appendices
	24th		Reorganisation Aut as about. J/84 became C/55, guns trans-ferred to 55th Bde R.F.D. Complete. Officers. Capt E.J. Bradden R.D. (Commanding) Lieut. H.J.S. Griffin " E.L. Carrol " C.C. Carver " R.S. Bowman. (4.5 How) A/85's howitzers Complete to 54th Bde R.F.A. Officers:- Capt L.V.G. Paul Commanding Lieut. C.R. Fenton 2Lieut. J.B. Bradbury 2Lieut. L.N. Trimby Lieut. A.D. Henry. Casualties - Nil.	

Army Form C. 2118

WAR DIARY
or
INTELLIGENCE SUMMARY
(Erase heading not required.)

Instructions regarding War Diaries and Intelligence Summaries are contained in F.S. Regs., Part II. and the Staff Manual respectively. Title Pages will be prepared in manuscript.

Place	Date	Hour	Summary of Events and Information	Remarks and references to Appendices
			Postings transfers &c. Lieut. C.W.K. White R.F.A. to 2 x Battery R.H.A. 2 " W.J. Barton " " W/15 Heavy T.M. Battery. Joined:— Lieut. E.W. Ashby from 15 D.A.C. 2 " J.N.C. Hutchinson " " 2 " J.S. Schofield " "	

[signature]
Lieut. Colonel, R.F.A.
Comdg. 84th Brigade, Royal Field Artillery.

3/6/16

WAR DIARY
or
INTELLIGENCE SUMMARY
(Erase heading not required.)

Army Form C. 2118

18 D/84 RFA Vol 1

Instructions regarding War Diaries and Intelligence Summaries are contained in F.S. Regs., Part II. and the Staff Manual respectively. Title Pages will be prepared in manuscript.

Place	Date	Hour	Summary of Events and Information	Remarks and references to Appendices
MARICOURT	30/4/16		Quiet day. 17BY & 14B fired in registration.	MARICOURT TRENCH MAP 62c NW1
	1/5/16		Quiet	WEP
	2/5/16			
	3/5/16			WEP
	4/5/16		10.5 cm How. shelling at intervals during the day. Saps & trenches opposite S.W end of Y wood. At 10.30 am we shelled trench 16BY in conjunction with other batteries a quick burst on enemy trenches in Y3 in retaliation to a similar form of procedure recently adopted by him. At 3.30 pm registered outposts Bn. HQ on dug outs at SUPPORT COPSE.	WEP
	5/5/16		At 3.37pm and 3.20 pm we fired on each occasion 16BY an ammunition with 18 Pdrs on JIGSAW COPSE in retaliation to the enemy shelling MARICOURT SUZANNE valley. The enemy At 7.pm again we shelled his trenches and dug outs at SUPPORT COPSE. retaliated at once on an outpost trench.	WEP
	6/5/16		Quiet	WEP
	7/5/16		Quiet. Lieut Fenton proceeded to England on 10 days leave.	WEP
	8/5/16		Quiet	WEP
	9/5/16		10.5 How again shelling throughout the day. Saps & trenches opposite S.W end of Y WOOD heavily	
	10/5/16		At 11 am a bombardment of Y3 was carried out. We fired 124 BY & damaged his trenches considerably. 10.5 Hows retaliated on same saps, to which we replied. 9 BY also 10.5 Hows fired from direction of GUILLEMONT on Battery Position during the day. 24 rounds 4.7mm gun from direction of CATERPILLAR WOOD fired on battery. Gr JACKSON wounded slightly in head previously WEP. 1875 Wt. W593/826 1,000,000 4/15 J.B.C. & A. A.D.S.S./Forms/C. 2118.

WAR DIARY
or
INTELLIGENCE SUMMARY
(Erase heading not required.)

Army Form C. 2118

Instructions regarding War Diaries and Intelligence Summaries are contained in F. S. Regs., Part II. and the Staff Manual respectively. Title Pages will be prepared in manuscript.

Place	Date	Hour	Summary of Events and Information	Remarks and references to Appendices
MARICOURT	11/5/16		Enemy 10.5" Howitzer again shelling x-rds and trenches opposite S.W. end of Y. WOOD. We retaliated expending 35 TSY. A&P. Also a certain 10.5 cm How from direction of CATERPILLAR WOOD active on the battery. A&P	MARICOURT TRENCH MAP 62 c NW 1.
	12/5/16		Enemy Hows & Trench Mortars active from 8am to 9.30 am on same trenches, but silenced by our 2" TMs & 18 Pdrs A&P	
	13/5/16		1 am hostile bombardment of Y2 and Y3 sectors and battery positions in MARICOURT - SUZANNE valley began. Telephone wires to both Sub: HQ cut. We opened fire on S.O.S. lines, viz, A29B 9515 - A23 D10 - A23 D8860 - A23 A 9310 at 1.15am. Message SOS Y2 received from R.Group RA at about 1.15am. Y3 HQ & B/149 (18 Pdr Bty, supporting Y3 where lines to Y3 HQ were also cut) unsuccessful at 2 am Y3 sent flares. SOS Y3. Battery ceased fire 2.45 am. 241 Rounds BX expended. Raid only partially successful. 1 German prisoner taken and several known to be killed hashmayday shells made effect felt at 1.25am goggles. Remainder of day quiet. Battery was shelled by certain 10.5 cm How from direction CATERPILLAR WOOD & also 77 gun, in same direction. Also 77 mm battery from direction of HARDECOURT opened fire with shrapnel. Remainder of day quiet. Rain. R&P.	
	14/5/16		Fine. Quiet. A&P	
	15/5/16			
	16/5/16			

1875. Wt. W593/826 1,000,000 4/15 J.B.C. & A. A.D.S.S./Forms/C. 2118.

WAR DIARY
or
INTELLIGENCE SUMMARY
(Erase heading not required.)

Army Form C. 2118

Place	Date	Hour	Summary of Events and Information	Remarks and references to Appendices
17.5.16			Line Quiet MO	
18.5.16			do MO	
19.5.16				
20.5.16			Registration	
21.5.16			235 Rounds fired in conjunction with 6" & 8" in afternoon from 4.15 & 4.30 Guns on enemy trenches from A23 c 8583 & A23 c 9077. 50 Rds 18 pdrs fired on Front line trenches from A23 c 8583 & A23 c 9077. 50 Rds on Bn MO	
22.5.16			Line Quiet MO	
23.5.16			Capt Paul proceeded on 10 days leave. Battery taken over by Lt Parke/BP	
24.5.16			Heavy shelling of Battery Position at 8-9.30 AM joint A27C & 6. 150 S. 9s being plentiful round Battery. Third small casualty MP Gr. Mn Dale 24.5.16 at 1.25C. The Battery changed to Brigade and instead of being A Battery 85 Brigade RFA under command of Col Wylie MO became D Battery 85 By RFA under command of Col Alton DSO MO	
26.5.16			Line Quiet MO	
26.5.16			do	
27.5.16			MO	
28.5.16				
29.5.16			Line quiet MO	
30.5.16				
31.5.16				

Rothery Capt RFA
cmdg D/84 427 H

WAR DIARY or INTELLIGENCE SUMMARY

Army Form C. 2118

84. R.F.A. Vol 12

Volume 12. part I.

84TH BRIGADE
Reg. No.
Date 5/7/16.
ROYAL FIELD ARTILLERY

June 1916.

Place	Date	Hour	Summary of Events and Information	Remarks and references to Appendices
ARDOEUVRES	JUNE 1st to 16th		Training continued at ARDOEUVRES. Brigade Sports were held on the 4th & most of the troops belonging to the 18th Div'l Arty. attended, also a large number of French troops and inhabitants were present.	
BATTLE QUARTERS	17th & 18th		The Brigade left ARDOEUVRES to take up its new position on the line on the NE of CORBIE on the night 18th. Something went slightly wrong and the Battn. did not do gun positions altogether during night. The wagon lines were in the Bois de Tailles — Battn. quarters and gun position were occupied during this period. Registration of targets with aeroplanes was also carried out. A/84, B/84 & C/84 R.F.A. were completing Obs. to Hill 10 Redout and One 4.5" Battery. The front allotted to the Bngde was known as Sector A1.	
BILLON VALLEY	23rd — 30th 6.30 pm		A Special programme of Artillery Bombardment and Infantry was set to carry the enemy lines by assault which consisted of bombardment for six (?) days. This Bngde was called 'V.W.X.Y.' Each Battery had a sheet of Artillery tasks to be and Battery of Ammunition Registers was carried out during the night. The great expenditure of Ammunition (approximately 1200 rounds per battery daily) in addition to the alarm contacts very heavy and took a man at the guns all day and night. Arguas which the Infantry went to assault were allotted for wire cutting and registration. Heavy barrages were also carried out in the 18" and 75" (?) Fired machine gun emplacements (5 Bns) were related to slow down the artillery.	

Volume 12 - page 2.

WAR DIARY
INTELLIGENCE SUMMARY
(Erase heading not required.)

Army Form C. 2118

June 1916 (Cont'd)

Place	Date	Hour	Summary of Events and Information	Remarks and references to Appendices
	23rd	10.30 p.m. Continued	For this operation each of 5, 18 par Batteries was given a definite strip of about 150 yards. Thus the Group covered about 750 yards which corresponded to the ground to be assaulted by 55th Inf. Bde. — One Battery (C/55th Bde R.F.A.) was further forward and was not unmasked until 2nd day. — D/61st was given a special job of dealing with strong points, O.P's, M.G. emplacements etc, when they were located. This zone of 750 yds extended west from the railway about 1,500 yds South of MONTAUBAN. 30th Div. on our right; 58th Bde covered by Centre Group consisting of 23rd Bde R.F.A. reinforced with 2 other Batteries was on our left. — Group H.Q. and all Batteries connected up by metallic circuit buried 1 foot deep; Batteries mostly observed from other O.P.'s constructed on main PERONNE — ALBERT ROAD, with forward observing stations in the front line for close wire cutting purposes. Group H.Q. and dug-outs quite near 55th Inf. Bde entirely situated. — The French were also preparing for offensive on our left, banks of the SOMME and had many gun positions in our vicinity. — These with the Pontoise heavy and field Batteries kept up an almost continual bombardment, and in some cases Batteries firing almost directly behind each other, a few casualties from prematures being the unavoidable result. — The average range of Batteries to the first line were about 3,000 yds, but the nearest forward that this was not too far as very little wire was left uncut on the day of assault. Many ruses to deceive the enemy as to day of attack were employed including heavy bombardment of front line, accompanied by both gas and smoke by day or night to suit the wind

WAR DIARY / INTELLIGENCE SUMMARY

Army Form C. 2118

Volume 12 page 3

84TH BRIGADE ROYAL FIELD ARTILLERY — Date 5/7/16

June 1916 contd.

Place	Date	Hour	Summary of Events and Information	Remarks
	29.6 to 30/6 (continued)		The groups were to increase the range entirely by time scale to correspond with the Infantry advance. Then to form a strong barrage in front of the final objective which barrage though invisible from any point was arrested several times with cessation of observation. Each Battery to be responsible for the same 150yds strip but to increase up to the final barrage, an advance of about one mile. The first part of the assault over about themes of trenches, about 800yds was timed to take 19 minutes, the remainder (after a halt of 1½ hours) to take about 80 minutes. The groups to make short lifts to keys about 100yds in front of the advancing infantry. The main lifts were arranged by Infantry Brigadier O.C. Groups to suit the needs of the ground etc. Minor lifts were arranged by Infantry Brigadier to notify their progress to the artillery. Infantry were provided with flags, discs, mirrors etc. Above Serre a Road from which passes the first 1000yds of the ground was for the most part invisible. But these devices were only to assist the advance could not account observation – the difficulties of smoke, dust etc being freely recognised as prohibiting accurate observation. — The 65th Bde to attack in a front of 2 Battalions, with one in support and one Brigade Reserve. The groups detailed one Officer with each leading Battalion & wij: —	
			B.s.R.R. above did a very good work, getting back free information by telephone as to the progress of the leading troops. The groups also detailed an Observing Officer's wij: —	

Volume 12, page 4

WAR DIARY or INTELLIGENCE SUMMARY

Army Form C. 2118

Summary of Events and Information — June 1916 (Contd)

who advanced 20 minutes after the first assault and succeeded in getting their accurate reports as to the shooting and establishing an advanced station of night in MONTAUBAN after the wires had been cut thereby shooting the barrage effect a fierce counter-attack from the north when the exhausted Infantry were less able to deal with it.

(Contd)

WAR DIARY
or
INTELLIGENCE SUMMARY
(Erase heading not required.)

Army Form C. 2118

Volume 12, pages

Instructions regarding War Diaries and Intelligence Summaries are contained in F.S. Regs., Part II. and the Staff Manual respectively. Title Pages will be prepared in manuscript.

Place	Date	Hour	Summary of Events and Information	Remarks and references to Appendices
			June 1916 (Contd)	
			Casualties during the month:— Officers Killed NIL Officers Wounded NIL	
			Other ranks " 2 Other Ranks " 4	
			Honours and awards:— Major G.W.S. Morris D.S.O.	
			Capt. L.J.C. Paul mentioned in despatches.	
			No 24490 Bomr. A. Meyers 7th Butchers Medal.	
			Signed, Lieut. Col. Commanding 64 F. Brigade R.F.A.	

18/VOL 13

84TH BDE.
R.F.A.

~~6th~~ July 1916.

WAR DIARY
or
INTELLIGENCE SUMMARY

Army Form C. 2118

Volume 13. Page 1. for July 1916.

Place	Date	Hour	Summary of Events and Information	Remarks and references to Appendices
BILLON VALLEY	1-7-16		The enemy's 1st-line was carried by Infantry assault in accordance with a prearranged programme. The objective of the 18th Div. was to take and consolidate MONTAUBAN ALLEY and POMMIERS REDOUBT. The Right Group consisted of 64th Bde. C/85. A/80 & C/83 and was commanded by Lieut Col. S.F.G. Blagg D.S.O. The Group supported the attack with intense bombardment on the front line of the German trenches prior to the assault and by a time table of lifts afterwards - The Infantry orders were the 55th Infantry Bde.	
		6.35am.	The attack commenced with an intense bombardment for 65 minutes.	
		7. A.M. to 10-30	Reports from F.O.Os. that our Infantry had made a good start, and at 10 a.m. that they had reached POMMIERS Redoubt and that the enemy was leaving MONTAUBAN by the Orchard few Batteries of the group were turned on to them -	
		12-30 pm	Bde Bde R.H.A. ordered move forward and occupy position North of PERONJE Rd. The Battery was in action ready to open fire at 2 p.m. Casualties during fire move were three Drivers and two horses wounded.	
		1-25pm	Our F.O.O. reports that our Infantry were crossing RIDGE on the line ORCHARD-TWING & BLIND ALLEY and that a large number of prisoners had been taken.	
		3.15pm	Our F.O.O. reported MONTAUBAN and Communication were established by telephone & visual.	
		7.0.	Reports that the 66th Infantry Bde. had gained the final objective and were in touch on both flanks -	
		9.30pm	The enemy made a strong counter attack on MONTAUBAN - S.O.S. was given and all Batteries took part & The attack was repulsed but the enemy kept up a heavy rifle during the night -	

Army Form C. 2118

WAR DIARY
or
INTELLIGENCE SUMMARY
(Erase heading not required.)

Instructions regarding War Diaries and Intelligence Summaries are contained in F.S. Regs., Part II. and the Staff Manual respectively. Title Pages will be prepared in manuscript.

Volume 13, page 2.

Place	Date	Hour	Summary of Events and Information	Remarks and references to Appendices
			For July 1916.	
HEAD QUARTERS BILLON VALLEY	July 2nd		The enemy continued to make counter attack on MONTAUBAN. Barrages were put up by the Brigade.	
	3rd		Very quiet day and very little shelling by the enemy. Several small parties of the enemy engaged while sending reinforcements into MAMETZ WOOD. Big gun left enemy ambulance wagon. Field or German lines & communication trenches.	
	4th		Found that the enemy's second line communication about 1000 rounds per day was captured by the troops. Enemy still MONTAUBAN way firing - small parties of Germans engaged & dispersed.	
	5th		ditto	
	6th			
	7th			
	8th		The Group was broken up & C/85 A/50 joined this respective Brigades.	
CARNOY	9th 10th 11th 12th 13th		Brigade Head Quarters, A/84, C/84, A/84 moved to forward position in CARNOY VALLEY. Fired on Support trenches of German second line, and engaged small hostile parties going to help the Germans in MAMETZ WOOD.	

WAR DIARY or INTELLIGENCE SUMMARY

Army Form C. 2118

Volume 13 page 3 for July 1916

Place	Date	Hour	Summary of Events and Information	Remarks and references to Appendices
CARNOY	14th	2.35 a.m.	Bombardment on enemy's 2nd line at LONGUEVAL commenced.	
		3. a.m.	Infantry commenced the assault and Artillery lifted to support trench 300 yards back.	
		3-5 a.m.	Barrage lifted 20 yards and fire continued for about 2 hours.	
		10 a.m.	Message received from our F.O.O. that BAZENTIN and LONGUEVAL were in our hands and brigade was not to move forward until our Cavalry and R.H.A had passed through MONTAUBAN.	
		4.30 p.m.	The Brigade moved forward to CATERPILLAR VALLEY, HEAD QUARTERS took up position in old German trench about 200 yards N. of MONTAUBAN on 16th and covered the front of the 9th Infantry Brigade.	
			Came under orders of 9th Div. and covered the front of the 9th Infantry Brigade.	
"	15th			
	16th		Assisted in an attack on the North end of LONGUEVAL	
	17th			
	18th	10 a.m.	We learnt that the 3rd Div. had gained LONGUEVAL less two strong points. Intermittent fire was kept up till 5 p.m. And started again about 7.20 p.m. Heavy fighting of a see-saw nature proceeded in DELVILLE WOOD during the evening which we supported.	

Casualties:- Lieut. C. ATKINSON and Lieut. A.J.D. HENRY both of 87th BATT
G.S.E. MANN Bty 87th Bn wounded.
Gr. D. McMANUS 96th Bn wounded.
Brigade and promoted Lieut.- Colonel.

WAR DIARY or INTELLIGENCE SUMMARY

Army Form C. 2118

Volume 13, page 4

For July 1916.

58TH BRIGADE
ROYAL FIELD ARTILLERY

Place	Date	Hour	Summary of Events and Information	Remarks and references to Appendices
	18			
	19th		Brigade was occupied in bombarding DELVILLE WOOD. Lieut. KEYMES and 2nd Lieut. ANDREWS were both killed by shell fire on the 19th. 2nd Lieut. PLATT and 2nd Lieut. C. WILLIAMS joined the Brigade from drafts to B/SH.	
	20th			
Bois Detailles	21st	2.30	Attack on LONGUEVAL and DELVILLE WOOD continued by the enemy. Our fire was very heavy. Shell and rifle fire. The Brigade was pressed out of LONGUEVAL and Lieut. Martin's Batt: instructions to their wagon lines. The withdrawal was carried out successfully without casualties.	
Ros Detailles	22nd			
ARQUEUVES	23rd		The Brigade marched to Bois de TAILLES, de TAILLES, Enemy at the	
	24th		Bivouac at the Army of ECKE. Billeting at ARQUEUVES - SPRYNDELL,	
HIRONDELLE	25th		when the Brigade entrained at PONT REMY for BAILLEUL and marched	
	26th			
	27th		to the remaining 8 miles.	
	28th			
ECKE	29th		In rest billets. The time was occupied in cleaning up and on re-equiping.	
	30th			
	31st			

5-8-16.

JA Connor
Lt Col RFA
Commdg 58th Bde RFA

Army Form C. 2118

18th Divn

84TH BRIGADE
Ref No.
Date 5/9/16
ROYAL FIELD ARTILLERY

WAR DIARY
INTELLIGENCE SUMMARY
(Erase heading not required.)

Instructions regarding War Diaries and Intelligence Summaries are contained in F.S. Regs., Part II. and the Staff Manual respectively. Title Pages will be prepared in manuscript.

Volume 14. page 1.   Summary of Events and Information for August 1916.

Place	Date	Hour	Summary of Events and Information	Remarks and references to Appendices
EECKE 1-5-16			In rest billets cleaning up and reequipping.	
LA-ARMÉE 2-5-16			Marched from EECKE to LA-ARMÉE (S.W. of ARMENTIERES) and took over the front of the New Zealand Division.	
	6-8-16 7-5-16		Front- Normal & quiet - Enemy shelling by the enemy with 10.5 c.m. B'ty had a direct hit on No 2 Gun Pit. Ft. Booth was Cpnl 92 Jolliffe wounded. Gun was knocked out of action with a broken Trail. This Battery moved into a fresh position the following day. Gun also hand a direct hit on a Gun Pit but had no casualties -	
	7-5-16 to 12-5-16		Nothing to report.	
	13-5-16		Had gas reminds to stop work on enemy's front line.	
	14 15 20		Nothing to report	
LAMORTIER 23rd	29th 30 31st		Handed over front to 146 R Bde and marched to wagon line at LA MORTIER and remained there till 29th B - Entrained at BAILLEUL and MERVILLE for new area. Detrained at DOULLENS and billeted at OUTRE-BOIS for the night and marched to new wagon Lines at BRICKFIELDS N.W. of ALBERT -	

5-9-16

J Crimes
Lt Col RFA
Cmnd'g 84 FA Bde

WAR DIARY
INTELLIGENCE SUMMARY
(Erase heading not required.)

Army Form C. 2118

Volume 15 page 1   September 1916.

Place	Date	Hour	Summary of Events and Information	Remarks and references to Appendices
BRICK-FIELDS (ALBERT)	1st		Received orders to be prepared to move at short notice to join the 25th Division who were preparing for special operations in front of Thiepval.	
USNA REDOUBT	2nd 3rd		Brigade moved forward pt. dawn and took up positions in MASH VALLEY. Brigade Head Quarters were established at USNA REDOUBT and registration of the new zone carried out. Brigade fired a series of lifts by a prepared Time Table to cover the attack made by the 75th Infantry Brigade on the enemy's second line in front of THIEPVAL.	
	4th		Rejoined 18th Div. Arty; and the Canadian Corps, took over position and Headquarters of the 5th Australian Brigade R.F.A. near OVILLERS and LA BOISELLES.	
LA BOISELLE	5th to 8th		Registration and protective barrage	
	9th		Brigade assisted in the support of the attack on the enemy's front line in front of COURCELETTE. The 1st Canadian Infantry Brigade carried out the attack supported by a succession of artillery lifts in accordance with 18th Div. Operation Order No.11. dep. 8th Sept 16.	
	10th 11th 12th 13th 14th		Ordinary Routine Work. The Brigade moved to new position in front CONTALMAISON on 13th Sept.	
CONTALMAISON	15th		The Canadian Corps resumed the attack northwards and took COURCELETTE. The Brigade assisted in the support by firing to a fixed Time Table of successive lifts of 100 yards every 3 minutes until the final barrage was reached. The rate of fire for the last 3 minutes was 6 rounds per gun per minute	
	16th		2/Lt. B.H. Austin 13/84th Bde R.F.A. Acts. R.F.A. wounded whilst doing duty as F.O.O.	

Army Form C. 2118

WAR DIARY
INTELLIGENCE SUMMARY
(Erase heading not required.)

Instructions regarding War Diaries and Intelligence Summaries are contained in F.S. Regs., Part II. and the Staff Manual respectively. Title Pages will be prepared in manuscript.

Place	Date	Hour	Summary of Events and Information	Remarks and references to Appendices
CONTALMAISON	17th		Vol. 15 page 2	
			Ordinary Routine Work.	
			B/84th. Battery heavily shelled by the enemy who knocked one gun out of action and set light to some ammunition. One man killed, two wounded on the occasion.	
	23rd to 25th		Battery moved forward to new position E of POZIERS, Brigade Headquarters remaining at CONTALMAISON. Registration and ordinary routine work.	
	26th		Assisted in the attack to clear up the situation NE of COURCELETTE	
	27th 28th		Supported the attack on the Enemys LE-SARS line	
	29th		Ordinary routine work	
	30th		Brigade moved to new position. Batteries in the NASH VALLEY and Brigade Headquarters in a dug out about 500 yds NW of USNA REDOUBT took over guns of 112 Brigade R.F.A.	
			The following awards were made for gallantry and devotion to duty:—	
			Lt. R.W. Deacon. B/84th. Military Cross.	Parchment Certificate
			Cpl. A.G. Shaw. B/84th. Military Medal + Certificate	Cpl. S.R. Cook. B/84th. Headquarters
			Bmbr. W.C. Morgan. C/84th. " "	Gr. J. Newman. " "
			Bmbr. R & Hall. B/84th. " "	V.J. Parker. B/84th. Bde R.F.A.
				Dis tinguished Conduct Medal.

4/10/16

J. Conner Lt Colonel
Commanding 84th Bde R.F.A.

War Diary
for
October 1916

84th Brigade
R.F.A.

Army Form C. 2118

WAR DIARY
or
INTELLIGENCE SUMMARY
(Erase heading not required.)

Instructions regarding War Diaries and Intelligence Summaries are contained in F. S. Regs., Part II. and the Staff Manual respectively. Title Pages will be prepared in manuscript.

[Stamp: 84TH BRIGADE ROYAL FIELD ARTILLERY Reg. No. S/1146 Date ...]

Summary of Events and Information for October 1916.

Volume 16 (page 1).

Place	Date	Hour	Summary of Events and Information	Remarks and references to Appendices
Old Gun Pits – OP6 Y.m.11.W. U.5.11.A	1st		Brigade took over the front of the 112 D'd R.F.A. and covered the 85th Infantry Brigade North of THIEPVAL.	
	2nd		Battery moved forward to new positions on the Eastern edge of AUTHUILLE WOOD. Brigade Head Quarters moved to DONNET POST.	
	3rd 4th	}	Digging Gun Pits.	
	6th	6.30	Covered 39th Infantry Brigade 6" carry out bombing attack on SCHWABEN – Brigade reached STUFF TRENCH.	
	6th	6.15	The Brigade fired Most Barrenets into the valley running through Pros Y Pl to present the Enemy from making for a counter attack.	
	7th 8th	}	Ordinary routine work starting Enemy's Gun positions.	
	9th		Round [?] in the attack that the NORTHERN End of SCHWABEN – The 16/16 Its to scarpe to silence but did not gain this objective – later in the day the Royals Reached the lost line on our right – in the system of STUFF REDOUBT.	
	10th 11th 12th 13th		Ordinary work.	
	14th		Supported the 118 Infantry Brigade in the attack on the Northern edge of SCHWABEN – The whole of the objective was gained and about 200 prisoners taken – The Brigade also rendered artillery aid to move to a forward position near MOGUET FARM – but the move was cancelled.	

WAR DIARY or INTELLIGENCE SUMMARY

Army Form C. 2118

Volume 16 (page 2)

Summary of Events and Information for Oct. 1916

84TH BRIGADE
Reg. No.
Date 5/11/16

Place	Date	Hour	Summary of Events and Information	Remarks and references to Appendices
BONNET POST	16th to 19th		Ordinary routine work.	
	20th	2.0ᵖ	The enemy made an ineffective Counter attack on SCHWABEN. The SOS was given and our barrage was reported as very effective. About 50 prisoners were taken.	
	21st		Supported the 11th Suffolks in their attack on STUFF-TRENCH:- Their attack was carried out in conjunction with the Division on our right – the whole objective of the Reserve Army was gained and about 1000 prisoners taken. The artillery communication going throughout the operations with the 11th Suffolks kept the Commander of 84th Bde in the Brigade & the Infantry. The question of 2ⁿᵈ gas Sub to 2ⁿᵈ Lt T.P. Phillips & two Signalmen was information received during these operations.	
	22ⁿᵈ to		Routine work. Preparing for operations which was to take place but on 31st put off being bad weather.	
	31st		The following Officers joined the Brigade:- Lt T. Pratt, Lt P.C. Inglis. 13/10 " E.C. Bourne. 9/10 " T.G. Griffiths. 9/10	Casualties 2ⁿᵈ Lt T.P. Phillips wounded 14 Other ranks wounded 1 " killed

5/11/16

JA Crowe
Lt Colonel, R.F.A.
Comdg. 84th Brigade, Royal Field Artillery

War Diary
for
November 1916

8th Bde. G.T.R.

WAR DIARY
INTELLIGENCE SUMMARY

(Erase heading not required.)

Army Form C. 2118

Volume ? 3/12/16

for November 1916

Place	Date	Hour	Summary of Events and Information	Remarks and references to Appendices
BONNET'S POST.	1st/11/16	9¹⁵	Ordinary routine work.	
	10th/11 11th/11 12th/11		Heavy intense bombardment commenced at 5.30 a.m. The 10th Corps & view to inflicting casualties and inducing the enemy to delay in manning his parapet on the day of attack. Inf: operations were delayed through bad weather. The Brigade bombarded R.B. 34 to R.19 d.65.	
	13th		Operation order No. 99 was carried out. 78th Div. R.A. supported the 39th Div. who attacked on the Enemy's defences South of the RIVR ANCRE and were & 3RD LINE between Squares R13 & 14 immediately South of BEAUCOURT SUR ANCRE. The attack was entirely successful and all objectives were gained in Coy's. A very adverse twenty four hours Rainbow Trenches was excellent. The Brigade covered the 118th Infantry Bde: Shooting was excellent throughout and communication was intact during the whole operation.	SEE BEAUCOURT Map 1/10000
	14th/11/16		Ordinary routine work. Batteries registered barrages for coming operations.	
	14th/5	6-10 a.m.	Operation Orders No. 104/5 (1st Div: bde) was carried out under Corps Conductor. There being snow on the ground and a thick November mist obscuring observation the whole of the day. The Brigade covered the 665 Infantry Bde: & 19th Div: in an attack on GRANDCOURT TRENCH & GRANDCOURT.	4/105
	16th/11 30/5		Ordinary routine work in watching & patrolling new front.	

O. Palmer Lieut Col
Commdy 548 Bde: R.F.A

Vol 18

Confidential
War Diary of
8th Brigade R.F.A.
From December 1st 1916. to December 31st 1916
(Volume VI)

Army Form C. 2118

WAR DIARY
or
INTELLIGENCE SUMMARY
(Erase heading not required.)

Volume 18 for December 1916

Place	Date	Hour	Summary of Events and Information	Remarks and references to Appendices
BONNETS POST	1st		Ordinary routine work.	
	2nd		The Brigade was relieved from the line by the 179th Brigade R.F.A. and moved to the wagon line SOUTH of ALBERT.	
ALBERT	3rd		The Brigade was reorganised and was made up to two 18 pdr. and one 4.6 Howitzer Batteries. The Right & Left Sections of C/84 were transferred to the C and D/84 respectively – The following Officers of the Brigade on formation:– Capt. L. J. Beddie, promoted Major & transferred to A/84 Bde R.F.A Lieut. G. M. Duff, Capt. " " A/84 " " R. R. Heiner, " " " B/84 " " L. J. Price, " " " C/84 "	H. Corner Lt. Col. R.F.A Comdg R.F.A 84 Bde R.F.A
	4th		The Brigade marched out to rest and arrived at GRAND LAVIERS.	
	6th			
GRAND LAVIERS	7th to 24th		Battery training.	
	25th		Inspection by II Corps Commander.	

www.ingramcontent.com/pod-product-compliance
Lightning Source LLC
Chambersburg PA
CBHW081433160426
43193CB00013B/2266